THE INCREDIBLE POWER OF PRAYER

The Incredible Power of Prayer was adapted from three previous books by Roger J. Morneau:

Incredible Answers to Prayer
More Incredible Answers to Prayer
When You Need Incredible Answers to Prayer

To order, call **1-800-765-6955.** For information on other Review and Herald products, visit us at www.rhpa.org

THE
INCREDIBLE
POWER OF
PRAYER

ROGER J. MORNEAU

REVIEW AND HERALD® PUBLISHING ASSOCIATION
HAGERSTOWN, MD 21740

This book was
Edited by Gerald Wheeler
Designed by Helcio Deslandes
Desktop technician: Shirley M. Bolivar
Cover design by Matthew Pierce
Typeset: 10/11 Palatino

PRINTED IN U.S.A.

04 03   12 11 10

R&H Cataloging Service
Morneau, Roger J., 1925-1998
        The incredible power of prayer.

        1. Prayer. I. Title.

                248.32

ISBN 0-8280-1329-2

CONTENTS

1

THIS IS THE
HOUSE OF DEATH

In December 1, 1984, I was on the verge of dying in the intensive care unit of the Greater Niagara General Hospital in Niagara Falls, Ontario. I had congestive heart failure and atrial fibrillation that the physicians could not reverse. As the cardiologist stated a few days later, if my wife had taken 20 minutes longer in getting me to the hospital, I would have been dead before arrival.

It came upon me unexpectedly. My wife, Hilda, and I were visiting her mother for the weekend. Our trip from central New York had been pleasant, and we had had an enjoyable evening with Mother. Retiring at 10:00 p.m., I felt unusually tired and slept comfortably till about 3:00 a.m., when I awoke with sweat pouring down my face. Although I realized that I was having some discomfort in breathing, I attributed it to the bedroom being overheated.

When I opened the window about two inches, the cool winter air immediately improved my condition.

However, I could not get back to sleep. I kept tossing in bed, and my breathing problem returned after a while.

I kept opening the window wider as breathing became more difficult, till by 7:00 a.m. I had it completely up.

After taking a shower, I became extremely tired and realized that something was definitely wrong with me. It took all the strength I could muster just to shave. Walking to the car required as much effort as if I were climbing a hill.

In the emergency room the staff quickly rigged me up with an oxygen mask, intravenous tubing dripping medication into my system, and a diagnostic monitor to check the activities of my heart. A cardiologist with the assistance of several nurses did everything they could to keep me alive.

A short while later they placed me in the intensive care unit, which was already filled to capacity. Because all the glassed-in chambers were occupied, they assigned me a bed in the open area close to the nurses' station.

I had, so to speak, a foot already in the grave, as my breathing had grown so shallow that I could hardly get any oxygen into my lungs. I now believed that I was going to die, and my conviction deepened when someone asked if I would like to have a minister come and see me. In my feeble condition I stated that I felt too sick to have anyone visit, except my wife, who was allowed to see me for 10 minutes every two hours. Besides, for almost 40 years I had made it a daily practice to seek out God and prepare myself to die.

While I realized that my condition was critical, I was also aware that a number of other people in the ward were struggling to hold on to life. "This is the house of death," I told myself.

The Presence of God
Thirty-six hours passed, and I was still alive and

now able to breathe without having the oxygen mask on all the time. My thoughts ascended to God in a melody of praise.

That Sunday evening the intensive care unit was in a state of great urgency, and the head nurse called for additional help to meet the situation. To my immediate right an elderly man appeared on the point of death as two nurses struggled to keep him alive. To my left a man in his 30s, already having had three heart attacks, stated that he was probably living his last days.

Lights flashed at the nurses' station with increasing frequency as the condition of a great number of patients worsened. Because of my close proximity to the station, I could hear comments that indicated that the condition of some patients was deteriorating and becoming desperate.

Not for myself, but for others, my thoughts ascended to God in prayer. For 39 years I had seen the power of intercessory prayer bring great blessings into the lives of many. One practice that I had formed early in my Christian life was to bring the spiritually sick, those who have had head-on collisions with sin and become spiritual and at times physical wrecks, to what I like to refer to as Christ's intensive care unit. The results had been rewarding, as many times I had seen my prayers answered before my eyes.

As I considered my Lord and Saviour in the Holy of Holies of the heavenly sanctuary ministrating in behalf of fallen humanity (Hebrews 8:1, 2), I found my heart soaring in thanksgiving for all the many blessings He had so compassionately bestowed on others in answer to my prayers. And my joy in the Lord was great as I reflected upon God's never-failing compassion toward me, a most undeserving human being.

Now I asked for the mighty power of the Holy Spirit of God to surround everyone with a spiritual atmosphere of light and peace and to restore them to health if it was His will. And to encourage my own Christian experience as I lay at the point of death, I asked God to allow me to see His healing touch at work in that ICU. Then I thanked the Great Physician, the Author of our being, for answering my prayers.

As I had discovered years before during a time when I had been personally involved in spirit worship, demonic spirits struggle hard before yielding their prey to the power of the Spirit of God. For about 15 minutes a large number of patients experienced increasing distress, and nurses actually ran to their aid. Then the medical staff's fears became reality as the heart of a Mr. Smith stopped beating.

The emergency beeper at the nursing station went into action, intensifying the sense of urgency. Immediately the head nurse asked over the PA system for all the doctors in the hospital to come and assist. Three physicians raced into the unit. A nurse on the run retrieved the resuscitator that had been left at the opposite end of the room.

About 10 minutes went by while the medical staff did all they could to restore him to life, with no success. In fact, one of them, leaving the room with his head down, came to the nurses' station and said to the nurse there, "The man is gone." Immediately, I appealed to the Lord of life in prayer, asking Him to restore Mr. Smith by the mighty power of the "Spirit of life" in Him (Romans 8:2), that great power that raised Lazarus from the dead. No sooner had I said amen than Mr. Smith regained consciousness and asked why so many people were in his room. He stated that he was extremely hungry, and asked if he could have some food.

Another of the physicians approached the station and told the nurse to order something from the kitchen, adding, "I have never seen anything like this in all my years."

My prayers had been answered in miraculous ways in that not only was Mr. Smith alive and feeling great, but also the peace of heaven now blessed those present in the intensive care unit. A state of quietness invaded the place. Nurses leisurely stood in the doorways of the glassed-in rooms as their patients actually fell asleep in the peace and comfort previously denied them. As for myself, I could feel the presence of God.

New Leases on Life

For long hours Hilda had been waiting to spend some of her allotted 10 minutes with me. About 10:00 p.m. she came in for the last time that day before returning to her mother's place for the night. During her stay in the waiting room of the ICU she had become acquainted with Mrs. Smith. The woman had been greatly disturbed over the condition of her husband, who—having given up hope—had actually declared that he wanted to die. Now Mrs. Smith told her of the marvelous—and even miraculous—change in her husband's physical condition, and of the drastic change of attitude he now possessed. Before he had said that he had wanted to die, but now he announced that he wanted to live.

Four days later I had the privilege of meeting the Smiths on the cardiac floor of the hospital. Their joy reflected the peace of God's love. Hilda has been corresponding with the woman, who has informed her that her husband has been in excellent health and hasn't missed any work since leaving the hospital. He retired, with the prospect of some good years ahead of him.

The day after Mr. Smith's recovery, the doctors discovered that some of their patients in the ICU were well enough to transfer out to other floors of the hospital. The condition of the cardiac patient on my left had changed so much for the better that the hospital moved him immediately, and he was exuberant with joy as he looked forward to a bright future. The elderly man on my right was like a different person. His physician was greatly surprised over the change in his condition, and declared him ready to be transferred the next morning if he continued to improve. It took place on Tuesday morning as anticipated. I was delighted to see my prayers answered before my eyes.

But as for myself, things didn't look good. In fact, at 8:00 a.m. on that Tuesday the cardiologist, answering my questions about my condition, indicated that the possibility of my getting out of the unit alive was extremely slim. Lab tests revealed that a virus had done irreparable damage to my heart.

With my heartbeats so irregular, I simply could not remain alive long in my current state. The doctor suggested one last treatment: to stop my heart with 50 volts of electricity, and restart it with a 200-volt shock. I signed the necessary papers to allow him to proceed. Later that afternoon the cardiologist informed me that the procedure had not helped.

My condition worsened as my lungs filled up with fluid. I realized that I wouldn't last much longer. That evening, although low physically, my mind was alert as I thought back upon almost six decades of living. Scene after scene passed through my mind, and my heart filled with gratitude to God as I saw the care He had exercised over me, even when I had no use for Him. Eventually my memory went back to when I was 7 years of age.

"He is alive! He is still alive!" Edmond, my older brother, shouted after shutting the power off and jumping through a remodeling opening in the floor to the basement below. I had tripped on a block of wood and fallen on a machine strap 14 inches wide. The strap drove a three-foot wheel deriving power from a nine-foot one with the help of a 350-pound tightener spinning on the strap. People had heard my shouts for help way up to the second floor even over the noise of the heavy machinery of the feed mill my father owned in eastern Canada.

If a three-inch steel shaft had not dislodged from its heavy mountings as a violent shock shook the building, I would have instantly perished. But instead the strap fell off the smaller wheel, which in turn caused the tightener to drop off the strap. I had fallen chest down on the strap, which carried me under the larger wheel, then up to the top, where I became wedged against a ceiling beam.

The wheel never slowed down until someone turned the power off. Almost all my clothes were torn off—a heavy winter jacket, a sweater, flannel shirt, and heavy underwear. My left arm was hanging down along the side of the wheel, and friction had worn the top of my hand and fingers down to the bones. For a while the doctor thought he might have to amputate, but I had praying parents who knew by experience the power of prayer in Christ, and all turned out well.

It took three days to repair the damage done to the machinery. According to the millwrights who worked on putting things back in running order, a supernatural force must have caused the damage. They stated that the weight of the tightener alone would have crushed every bone in my body and the machinery wouldn't have slowed down a bit, much less cause that heavy steel shaft to slip out of place. The force that jolted it free, they estimated, had to be equivalent to the impact of an object of one ton.

"O that men would praise the Lord for his goodness, and for his wonderful works to the children of men!" (Psalm 107:8).

Yet as I thought over my past, I recalled at age 12 how bitter I had become toward God when my mother was lowered in her grave. In my grief I could not adjust to the idea that a good God would allow the suffering of humanity to go on and on, and do nothing to end it. I lost belief in Him and the supernatural. In my late teens I read the works of infidels, then some of Charles

Darwin's writings, and to top it all, Thomas Henry Huxley's works convinced me that man was a direct descendant of apes. By the age of 21 I considered myself to be an atheist, having rejected all the Catholic beliefs I had ever had, and denied the existence of God. Then unexpectedly I had a most shocking experience with the supernatural. And little did I know that God was watching and caring for me.

It was 1946 in Montreal, Canada, and I met a wartime buddy who had become a member of a society that claimed to communicate with the spirits of the dead. I became involved in their practices, and before long my friend and I were led into a secret society who worshiped super intelligent, beautiful beings whom they referred to as gods. In fact, their worship room contained numerous beautiful paintings of spirits who had materialized, were photographed, then had paintings made of them.

During that time I was working for a Jewish embroidery firm. One of the owners asked me to do him a favor. He had just hired a man whose religious beliefs puzzled him. The boss wanted me to find out what denomination he belonged to. In the process I became deeply interested in what the Bible had to say about the supernatural world of spirits.

A couple days went by; then the spirits informed the high priest of our society that I was studying the Bible and that the gods were furious. Within a few short days the group's leaders offered a $10,000 contract on my life. But the spirits advised that the killing should not be done by anyone outside of the society, and that members should dispose of me by shooting me at a convenient time. The spirits would endow three volunteers with the gift of clairvoyance, enabling them to know where I was at all times. Again the Lord delivered me from an early grave. (A detailed account appears in my book *A Trip Into the Supernatural* [Review and Herald, 1993].)

Now, in that hospital bed, although my body was failing, my mind was still clear and sharp. I realized more than ever before the power contained in God's holy Word, as Psalm 103:10-14 (scriptures memorized years back) went through my mind: "He hath not dealt with us after our sins; nor rewarded us according to our iniquities. For as the heaven is high above the earth, so great is his mercy toward them that fear him. As far as the east is from the west, so far hath he removed our transgressions from us. Like as a father pitieth his children, so the Lord pitieth them that fear him. For he knoweth our frame; he remembereth that we are dust."

Hope, encouragement, and faith sprang into my heart. With joy I recalled that bright sunny day during April 1947 when I was baptized in Montreal, Canada.

In the autumn of that year the Lord greatly enriched my life when on September 20 Hilda and I united in marriage. My young bride was a devout woman who understood the power of intercessory prayer, and who for four decades has been instrumental in securing from on high the divine help that has kept Satan from bringing me to an early grave.

Now becoming extremely tired, I asked the Lord to give me some rest, and I would converse with Him in prayer at 3:00 a.m. when the nurses would awaken me for my medications.

The Hour of Deliverance

Since 1946 when I had had that unique encounter with demonic spirits, I had experienced moments of fright as I thought about the future. Then the Spirit of God would bless me by leading me to read two portions of Scripture: Revelation 12:11, "And they overcame him by the blood of the Lamb," and Romans 8:38, 39, "I am persuaded, that neither death, nor life, nor angels, nor principalities, nor powers, nor things present, nor things to come, nor height, nor depth, nor any other creature, shall be able to separate us from the love of God, which is in Christ Jesus our Lord."

In that way I learned to fortify myself in the merits of the sacrificial blood of Christ. And in addition, I made it a part of my morning devotions to review the events of that sacrifice by reading Matthew 27:24-54. Such practices have removed all fear of the destroyer, and served to surround me with a spiritual atmosphere of light and peace. So, after taking my medications at 3:00 a.m., I reviewed mentally those verses of Scripture just mentioned. I presented before my great High Priest in the Holy of Holies of the heavenly sanctuary, my personal needs, telling Him that if my pilgrimage through this land of the enemy was coming to an end, it was OK with me, seeing that it is the common lot of humanity to go to the grave sooner or later. But I added, "Lord, if it be pleasing in Thy sight, I would appreciate Your honoring the prayers of the many persons who are praying for my recovery, so that they may see them answered, and their Christian experience strengthened. If so, then bless my damaged heart with the power of the Spirit of life in Thee, that great power that raised Lazarus from the dead, and impart to me strength and energy sufficient to meet the needs and demands of this day."

From experience I had learned that when in faith we take hold of His strength, He will change—wonderfully change—the most hopeless, discouraging outlook, if it is our heavenly Father's will. As I closed my morning devotions an assurance rested upon me that all was well, regardless of what the outcome might be.

I slept soundly till 6:00 a.m. when the lab nurse came to draw some blood. By 7:30 the cardiologist approached my bed with a smile on his face that let me understand that his concern over my condition had lessened. He began by saying that things were looking up, and that a great change for the better had taken place, something he could hardly believe. Pointing to the heart monitor, he said, "The last time I saw you, the monitor was indicating that your heart was beating anywhere between 145 and 185 times per minute. Now it's in the 80s. If your condition holds this good till 3:00 this afternoon, I will have you transferred to the cardiac unit of the hospital."

By 3:00 p.m. my improved condition was holding, and an orderly wheeled me into a lovely room with the sun shining in brightly. Suddenly I realized that my enjoyment of life had grown as never before. Even the dirty city snow somehow awakened in me a new sense of appreciation as I watched the little sparrows bounce around on it.

The Lord had seen me through "the valley of the shadow of death," and I had reached new heights of understanding about the power of intercessory prayer. And though I had almost passed through the portal of the tomb, I now valued the experience, realizing that the Lord of glory had been at my side through the presence of His Spirit in a way that I had never known before.

Almost a week to the hour that I had been admitted to the emergency room, I walked out of the hospital on my own two feet. Those feet may not have moved very fast, but they did carry me again to the world outside, and that was wonderful.

2
GOD PROTECTS HIS CHILD

God used a number of experiences to prepare me so that He could then bless others through my intercessions. They helped me to see both the importance and power of intercessory prayer.

The first of these experiences happened in the wintertime. For a number of days I had been studying the biblical concept of faith. While Scripture speaks of vast numbers of people having had their lives ruled by distrust of God and unbelief, it also reveals how certain persons acquired a living faith by developing an unfaltering trust in our heavenly Father, and in the power of His Holy Spirit. I decided to keep thanking the Lord for all the many times in my life when His Spirit had given me faith, and asked Him to increase it.

That particular morning in my devotions I read the experience of Philip in Acts 8, where an angel told him to go south of Jerusalem on the road to Gaza. There he saw the treasurer of Candace, queen of Ethiopia, sitting in his chariot reading a scroll of Isaiah. Then the Spirit of God said to Philip, "Go near, and join thyself to this chariot."

As a result, a baptism took place, and the Bible says that "when they were come out of the water, the Spirit of the Lord caught away Philip." And he found himself at Azotus, a little town about 20 miles from where he had left the Ethiopian eunuch.

Reading the story, I said to myself, *What exciting times those days were when the Spirit of God was so close to people.* And through the rest of that day I meditated on the biblical story.

In those days I was a salesman, and that evening I had a 9:00 p.m. appointment with a building contractor living on a rural road about four miles west of Castile, New York. Our home was in Curriers, about seven miles north of Arcade. To avoid a route that would have forced me to go east in a roundabout way, I had gotten instructions to go cross-country on some county roads that would supposedly save me a lot of travel time. Unfortunately, it didn't. I got lost three times because of the constant crossroads, and I made wrong turns. It meant stopping and asking directions at farms, and I arrived almost an hour late.

On my way there I realized that my gas gauge had dropped rather low, but reasoned that the best thing to do was to fill the tank in Castile afterward. We got involved talking business, and time flew by. When I had finished writing up an order and was ready to leave, my watch indicated almost midnight. By then the thought of getting gasoline had left me. The contractor, desiring to save me going into Castile in order to take Route 39, a state road that would carry me west into Arcade and home, suggested that I drive three miles west from his residence, then take a left that would get me directly onto Route 39.

I was reluctant to go that way, but he said I couldn't make a wrong turn because of a huge landmark at that intersection. As I stepped out on the porch, the cold chilled me instantly. He looked at his thermometer, which read five degrees below zero.

"I hope you have a good battery," he said.

"Yes, sir. One of the best for winter driving." Waving goodbye, I left. Because of the bitter cold, it took longer than usual to get heat into the car, and it absorbed all my attention. I had traveled about five miles when all of a sudden the engine began to lose power. A glance at the gas gauge told me the tank was empty. Terror struck my mind as I realized that the last farm I had passed was more than a mile away, and no more were in sight.

Like a flash I saw myself in a hospital bed with my toes cut off. You see, when I was 17 years of age, I froze all my toes one morning in northern Quebec when the temperature had gone down to -42° F. I spent five months in the hospital. The flesh turned black and actually fell off my toes. Afterward I had a number of operations, skin grafts, etc. And the day of my discharge the surgeon who had worked on my feet sat me down and stated that I should no longer live in that part of the world. He believed that my feet would quickly freeze if exposed to the cold, and that the only thing that could be done then would be to amputate.

Now in a burst of fear I cried out, "Dear Jesus, please help." Many times before when certain destruction stared me in the face, I had made that call for help, and Jesus had never failed me. Immediately a great calm came over me. But the car was still slowing down.

"Forgive me for being so panicky, seeing that You have never failed me," I prayed. "O Lord, I know that the Spirit of God that transported Philip 20 miles so long ago can get me and this car over those hills into Curriers if He so chooses. Dear Jesus, may the Spirit of God that controls the atoms please fuel this car so it will take me home without stopping. Thank You, Lord, for Your help."

It was almost as if something hit the back of my automobile, and it shot forward; then the motor started to accelerate and hummed like never before. The speedometer climbed and when it reached the speed limit I had to release my foot from the pedal, as the vehicle kept dashing ahead. Eagle Hill—which I had never climbed without the transmission shifting down—I now sped up in high gear. Jubilantly I praised the Lord for His miracle-working power.

I began quoting verses of Scripture, such as Psalm 107:1, 2, and 8: "O give thanks unto the Lord, for he is good: for his mercy endureth for ever. Let the redeemed of the Lord say so, whom he hath redeemed from the hand of the enemy." "O that men would praise the Lord for his goodness, and for his wonderful works to the children of men!"

Praising the Lord with my whole heart and at the same time crying for joy, I felt the words of Psalm 105:1-5 had never sounded so wonderful. "O give thanks unto the Lord; call upon his name: make known his deeds among the people. Sing unto him, sing psalms unto him: talk ye of all his wondrous works. Glory ye in his holy name: let the heart of them rejoice that seek the Lord. Seek the Lord, and his strength: seek his face evermore. Remember his marvellous works that he hath done; his wonders, and the judgments of his mouth."

After I pulled into the driveway, up a small grade, and past the side entrance of our house, the car stopped. It did not reach the garage. Turning the ignition off, I ran into the house, surprised to see the lights on in the kitchen.

About 11:45 p.m. Hilda had awakened, and realizing that I was not home yet, got on her knees and prayed for God's loving care over me. As I entered, she knew that something great and wonderful had happened. "You look excited. What's the good news?"

I recounted how the Spirit of God had brought me

home 27 miles without any gas in the tank. We had a praise session to the Lord that probably lasted an hour, then went to bed but could not sleep most of the night, as we kept talking about my experience.

In the morning I tried to start the car, but it would not. We had to fetch gasoline from the neighbor's farm to get it going.

Facing Death and No Time to Pray

Nothing prepares a person for sincere heartfelt prayer as the threat of death. And I have found by experience that nothing calms fear as well as memorizing verses of Scripture that tell of God's deliverance in ages past. During times of need the Spirit of God fortifies the mind with the power inherent in the Word of God.

I have had experiences that would have driven me crazy were it not that I had fortified my mind in the Word of God, and trusted the Lord to carry me through whatever He would allow to come my way.

In late March, about two months after the previous incident, we had a lot of snow in the western New York area. In Wyoming County around the Arcade-Rushford area, snowplows had piled up mounds in some places as high as 10 feet. But the rigor of winter was beginning to abate, the sun was gaining strength, and the days were getting longer.

One particular evening while I traveled home I occupied my time memorizing 2 Chronicles 16:9: "The eyes of the Lord run to and fro throughout the whole earth, to shew himself strong in the behalf of them whose heart is perfect toward him." By then I neared Rushford, driving at a reasonable rate of speed and slowing down before each turn in the road, as it was impossible to see if any vehicles were coming around the corner.

Suddenly I came upon a stretch of road that was quite slippery, as some of the snow had thawed during the day, then refroze when the sun went down, leaving large patches of ice. It was impossible to brake lest I lose control of the car. Touching neither brake nor accelerator, I let the car roll into the curve with the hope that nothing approached from the opposite direction.

As I rounded the corner I saw a large horse standing in the middle of the road. There was no way to avoid hitting it. My hands froze on the steering wheel, and all I could say in a call for help was "Dear Jesus." Instantly some force, which I believe to be the Spirit of God, since I felt the exact same presence that night two months before, wrestled the steering wheel out of my hands and directed the car toward the front legs of the horse. Just a moment before impact the animal reared up on its hind legs, and I slumped in my seat to avoid the hoofs hitting me in the face through the windshield.

They cleared the car probably by one or two inches. A short distance down the road I managed to bring the car to a stop and give my pounding heart a couple minutes to recover and at the same time send forth a prayer of thanks.

Realizing the danger to other motorists, I drove to the first house down the road to see if the horse belonged there. When I explained what had happened, the man stated that the animal belonged to a neighbor and was kept indoors during the winter months. Picking up the phone, he contacted the owner, who declared that his horse had been in its stall a half hour ago when he had completed his evening chores. However, he would check and call right back.

A few minutes later the message came that in some mysterious way the horse had gotten out. The stall door was wide open, the barn door was ajar, and the animal was gone.

Neither man could figure out how it could have taken place. Nobody could have reached the barn without someone seeing him, since the driveway faced a large picture window in the kitchen where the family had been at the time. "It's strange, strange," they said.

My wife and I had another praise session to our heavenly Father. Death had stared me in the face, but the eyes of the Lord had been upon me, and His Spirit brought deliverance. That incident helped me to grow in knowledge of God.

Lamentations 3:22-26 contains special words of hope and assurance of God's loving care over those who place their lives in His protection. "It is of the Lord's mercies that we are not consumed, because his compassions fail not. They are new every morning: great is thy faithfulness. The Lord is my portion, saith my soul; therefore will I hope in him. The Lord is good unto them that wait for him, to the soul that seeketh him. It is good that a man should both hope and quietly wait for the salvation of the Lord."

Many times over the years my heart has lifted up to God in thanksgiving whenever the Spirit of God has brought me out of impossible situations.

Truck Crash

For almost 20 years I worked in telephone directory advertising sales (yellow pages) for both the Bell and Continental telephone systems in Ohio, New York, and Pennsylvania. For the last five of those years, I was division sales manager for the Mast Advertising and Publishing firm of Overland Park, Kansas, publishers of directories for Continental Telephone and other independent telephone companies. I had charge of directory people in the Northeast Division, covering an area of eight states.

Yearly I traveled anywhere between 25,000 and 45,000 miles. I was on the road in rainstorms, snowstorms, dense fog, and other unfavorable conditions. Frequently I saw cars hurtling at me that were undoubtedly driven by drunks or individuals with their minds spaced out on drugs.

To be crushed in a car on a highway is something that doesn't attract much media attention in this day and age, but to be smashed in a car in a Sears parking lot could get front-page attention.

In December 1971 I was working on the Watertown, New York, telephone directory. For a few nights it had been exceedingly cold for that time of the year, and one morning I wanted to assure myself that my battery would not fail me, so I proceeded to the Sears auto department to have it checked.

It was a busy morning in the service department, undoubtedly brought about by the cold spell that had taken many by surprise. Being unable to bring the car indoors (the bays were filled), the service manager brought a tester out to the car, performed the necessary checks, and announced that the battery would carry me through another winter without any problems.

Meanwhile a large tractor-trailer loaded with 27 tons of cargo had parked sideways behind my car while the driver went inside the store to get unloading instructions. My car faced the building, making it impossible to get away. At the time I was driving a small Saab. The manager suggested that I back up under the body of the huge trailer, as there was sufficient room to do so. He would guide me in the maneuver.

The truck motor was turned off and the brakes set, or otherwise it would have rolled down the hill, since the parking lot was on a steep incline.

Slowly I backed under the trailer while the service manager directed me. When I had all of the car under the trailer except the motor, suddenly I felt that same feeling of urgency that I had experienced in previous emergencies. I remember bringing the gearshift out of reverse position; then what seemed to be a powerful and sudden push propelled the car forward. If I had not had my foot on the brake I would have hit the building. Even with that lunge forward, the vehicle did not get completely out of the path of the truck that suddenly shot backward, hitting the rear bumper and knocking the taillight off the fender. The blow shoved the back part of the car sideways about three feet.

The people who had been watching me back up under the trailer ran to the car to see if I was all right. Although shaken some, I was not hurt. They kept repeating, "Are you all right? Man, are you ever fortunate. You were almost killed. How did you get that car forward so quickly? How did you know that the truck was going to roll? How were you able to stop the car from going into the brick wall?" One elderly woman declared, "Your angel saved your life. God must certainly love you a lot." A man said, "Fellow, you were almost crushed flat into that car. Do you realize that?"

The tractor-trailer damaged several cars, jackknifed, then stopped as it demolished the back half of a large Chrysler. The driver of the rig appeared on the scene in time to see his vehicle crash into the last car. Unable to believe his eyes, he emphatically declared that he had the truck in forward gear and that the emergency brake was on.

The owner of the Chrysler was furious. He and his wife had gotten out of the car just a few seconds before the accident and were walking up to the store; they had to run out of the way to avoid being hit. He began accusing the driver of being many unflattering things, including being an idiot for leaving a truck standing without the brakes secured properly. Determined to check them there and then, he started for the cab, but the driver refused to let anyone enter it and stayed out of it himself until the Watertown police could get there and make an accident report.

A great number of people gathered quickly, everyone curious to know what had taken place. They were amazed that I had escaped certain death. When the police arrived they tried to disperse the crowd and clear the way so that traffic could move, but the people didn't want to leave.

One of the officers climbed into the cab of the truck to examine the controls. He stated to his partner that the ignition was off and the gear shift was in neutral, and the light on the dashboard indicated that the brakes were on. Naturally he couldn't figure out what had happened that would have allowed the truck to roll as it did.

When he prepared his report I was the first one he interviewed. At the close, he said, "Mr. Morneau, you are a very lucky person in the fact that you are alive at this moment. A second longer under that trailer, and you would not be here making an accident report. Instead you would have made the front page of the evening paper, and I can imagine how that would read."

As I drove away, the words "It is of the Lord's mercies that we are not consumed, because his compassions fail not. They are new every morning" went through my mind.

3
JESUS'
INTENSIVE
CARE UNIT

A s I studied the power and impact of intercessory prayer, I concluded that one needs to be fitted in a special way to conduct a successful prayer ministry.

The most important thing we must receive is a mind like that of Christ. "Let this mind be in you, which was also in Christ Jesus" (Philippians 2:5), Paul said. When Eutychus "fell down from the third loft, and was taken up dead," he could say, "Trouble not yourselves; for his life is in him" (Acts 20:9, 10). He had seen his silent prayers answered before his eyes so many times that he knew without a doubt that God had heard the cry of his heart as he ran downstairs to the youth.

I can imagine him saying, "Dear Jesus, Thou art Lord of the impossible. Please turn this misfortune around so that Thy people will exalt Thy great name in a praise session that will continue the rest of their lives as they think back upon this event. Thank You, Lord, for Your love and Your grace."

So I began to pray for the Holy Spirit to impart the mind of Christ to me. But after a while the Spirit of God led me to understand that I didn't really know what I was asking for, and that God cannot really answer us when we stay on the level of generalities. From that time on my prayers took on a whole new meaning. No longer did I use vague expressions, such as "Lord, please bless this person." Instead I asked that God would bless a person in a specific way, so that I would then be able to see that He was answering my prayers as the very things I had asked for took place before my eyes. In other words, I was learning to pray meaningful prayers, and to understand that we cannot rush through them. Unhurried, meaningful prayer is time consuming and at first unappealing to the human mind, but I discovered that it produces great results.

As I continued praying to receive the mind of Christ, it became clear that a mind like His would mean that I would think as He thinks and feel as He feels about life on our fallen planet until I in turn began to act as He would if He were in my place. In other words, I would find myself having a lifestyle patterned after His own righteous mind.

While my reasoning was to a large extent correct, I did not really understand the vastness of the blessings that await us through the character of Christ. I had just touched upon only a very small part of what constitutes the mind of Christ. As I read further, my understanding grew. I concluded that I could not expect to operate successfully in a world of sin with less grace than what Jesus had prayed for and received during His life on earth.

Now I added to my daily petitions to God a request for a fresh baptism of the Holy Spirit. I asked that the Spirit of God would enable me to obtain a greater knowledge of my Lord and Saviour, and the power of

His resurrection, something that the apostle Paul had craved for (Philippians 3:10). And to my great amazement, things began to take place in my life that I had not expected and would never have thought possible.

During the middle 1960s, while I worked on the Hudson, Ohio, telephone directory, God especially blessed my Christian experience and began to make of me a channel for His influence. A few months previous I had changed my line of work by going into telephone directory advertising sales. After nearly a month at the training school in Dayton, Ohio, the company assigned me to work on small telephone directories in New York state to gain experience. Soon they put me on larger projects, and before long they appointed me to the Hudson, Ohio, telephone directory, a geographical area covered by the Mid-Continent telephone system.

In addition to business accounts assigned to me in the local Hudson telephone area, I had to contact business firms located in the cities of Akron, Kent, and Ravenna. The work was interesting, but at the same time rather demanding. It challenged one's creativity to make up ads that would meet each firm's needs. If the ads you made did not bring in customers, the next year the owner would cancel them.

Each evening we would prepare ads designed to be both appealing and informative. It took six individuals three weeks to make up the Hudson directory, while in the case of the Buffalo, New York, telephone book 43 persons spent six months covering that market area.

Time was at a premium in that one had to handle a certain number of accounts each day in order to close the directory on time. Visiting the business in person could be time-consuming if advertisers carried ads of many classifications and had acquired different product lines. That required a change of copy to put in the new information and to delete what was no longer needed.

One factor that had a lot to do with one's success

was finding the business owners in their establishments. If they were out, it meant calling back later, which consumed valuable time and kept you from seeing some of your other customers. All one needed to get into a crisis situation was to have the misfortune of having many of the owners out two or three days in a row. Besides, when you get pressed for time, tension mounts, and it's hard to operate effectively.

Because of the fact that businesspeople face great pressure, if the yellow pages representative can't maintain a cheerful, pleasant, and diplomatic attitude, he may lose advertising revenue or the contract altogether. Early in the game I learned that I needed to pray on the run in order to succeed. I quickly understood that I needed special blessings from God to keep from burning out under pressure.

One morning I called on an automobile body repairing and painting shop. As I reviewed the copy in his display ad, the owner stated that he needed a few days to make up his mind, as he was contemplating closing the business (if he did, he would cancel his ad). I asked why he would do a thing like that, when he had what seemed to be a very progressive operation.

"I might as well tell you about my problem. Would you please close the office door?"

As I sat down again, he said, "I don't know why I am telling you this, when I have told no one else. I have a bad situation at home that is getting worse by the day. My wife and I are not getting along anymore, and I have come to the point that I feel like closing this shop, moving to California with my 16-year-old son, and filing for divorce. That's why it's so difficult for me to make a final decision about my advertising."

Considering the pressure of my schedule and the training I had received, the right thing for me to have done in such a case would have been to cancel the man's advertising (I would need his signature to cancel) and to explain that I could put it back in if he called the telephone business office before the date that the book went to the printers. That would have saved me the trouble of coming back, which would have enabled me to use my time selling advertising to other business firms.

But I didn't do that, because I kept hearing those words, "Not for Himself, but for others, He lived and thought and prayed." I felt strongly that I should have the man unload his burden while I silently prayed for him. Then I asked, "Do you mind telling me how things got so bad?"

"It began about three years ago," he said, "shortly after we moved into our beautiful new house. My wife began to place silly demands upon me. She complained that I was not giving her enough of my time, and that I loved my business more than her. I agreed that I did spend a lot of time managing the business—to serve the public is time-consuming. And I tried to explain that in order to acquire all the things she had asked for, I had to work long hours and there was no getting around that fact. But somehow she could not understand that, and kept nagging and accusing me of being hard-hearted. The time came when she got enraged to the point of throwing dishes on the floor."

"Have you thought of getting professional counseling on the matter?"

"Yes, we went that route last year. It helped for a while, but her anger kept coming back. I tell you, she is not the same person I have known for so many years. She can be real sweet, then for no reason at all her personality changes, and she becomes mean and ugly. One thing I do know for sure is that I cannot continue living like this."

I would have liked to talk to him about God, but I could not because in training school the instructors had told us in no uncertain words that it was against company policy to talk politics or religion with yellow pages customers, and that company time is strictly for conducting business.

Instead I suggested that I would return in two weeks to give him a chance to decide about his yellow pages ad. He felt good about that, and as I left his place of business, I mentioned that I would remember him and his wife in my prayers. The man thanked me for my interest in his problem.

As I was driving to my next call, thinking about his difficulties, I felt a deep concern for the couple's well-being, something I had never experienced before toward complete strangers.

Now I realized that the way I felt was undoubtedly a result of Christ's imparting His compassionate love to me by the Holy Spirit in answer to prayer. A sudden desire to stop and pray for them possessed me as I passed a supermarket. Turning into the parking area, I drove to the back, where I turned the motor off. As I did, I said to myself, "I only wish that our Lord had a special intensive care unit for those devastated by the ravages of sin and oppressed by Satan."

My wife, Hilda, a nurse, was at the time working in the intensive care unit of a large hospital. A couple days previously we had talked about her work, and I had been fascinated by the care and dedication the nurses exercised toward their patients. I longed for similar spiritual help for those facing crises.

Taking my Bible out of my briefcase, I opened it at the twenty-seventh chapter of Matthew and read some about the Crucifixion. Then I pleaded in prayer the merits of the blood that Christ had shed on Calvary as the reason that the man I had just talked to, and his wife, should receive divine help.

God was leading me into a prayer ministry that would bless the lives of a great many persons, bringing them the peace of His love in a cruel world.

The time I had taken to have the businessman tell

me about his problems God helped me to make up that
afternoon. On every call I found owners at their business, in a good mood, and interested in having a larger
and better yellow pages program. At the end of the day
I totaled my increase and found it to be the best day in
net revenue I had ever had. It greatly pleased my supervisor, who asked me to pass on the secret of my success
to the other advertising representatives. I did by saying
that the great Monarch of the galaxies had crowned my
efforts with His divine blessing.

To secure divine help for the body shop man and his
wife, I lived the next two weeks a bit differently. Each
night I set the alarm clock 15 minutes earlier than usual
because I wanted to begin each new day with prayer for
the couple. After reconsecrating and rededicating my
life to God, I would intercede with Him in their behalf.
With the Bible opened at the Crucifixion chapter,
Matthew 27, I pleaded the merits of Christ's blood as
the reason that they should receive special help in their
daily lives.

My first intercession went something like this:
"Precious heavenly Father, I wish to thank Thee first
for having allowed Christ to come and live among us
and then purchase our redemption at such a great cost.
In addition, I desire to express my appreciation in that
You have honored me so greatly before the inhabitants
of the galaxies and the angels of heaven by having
made me a member of Jesus' resistance forces in a sin-
occupied world.

"I also rejoice over the fact that You have revealed to
us the many functions the Holy Spirit can perform to
work out human salvation, and close Thy mission on
earth with power and great glory. Gracious Father, because the pen of inspiration has referred to Thee as 'the
Father of infinite pity,' I do not hesitate to bring to Your
attention the lives of Mr. and Mrs. A.

"I realize that they have been under the constant attack of Satan and have struggled with depressing thoughts and experiences. Yes, their lives are in a sad state of affairs, and I refuse to sit back and do nothing while God's enemies increase their efforts to defeat Christ's work in man's behalf, and to fasten souls in their snares.

"I plead, O Lord, the merits of the blood the Lord of glory shed on Calvary for the remission of sins for the salvation of this couple. You know, Father, that I do not hesitate to ask for the divine power of the third person of the Godhead to rebuke Lucifer and his spirit associates from controlling human lives. When I was a spiritist, the persevering supplications of Cyril and Cynthia Grosse in my behalf opened the way for Thy Holy Spirit to shelter me from demonic activities for a whole week, making it possible for me to receive Bible studies and accept Christ as my Lord and Saviour.

"So, Father, may Thy Holy Spirit overshadow Mr. and Mrs. A this day, surrounding them with a spiritual atmosphere of light and peace, allowing them to make intelligent decisions in this present life and for eternity. I know, Lord, that You will not force anyone into a particular course of action, but You are able to help people in making right decisions.

"Nor do I hesitate to ask for mighty miracles of divine grace to take place in their lives, since Christ has already paid the price for any and all blessings that heaven can bestow.

"As for myself, as an intercessor in opening the way for the third person of the Godhead to move in mighty ways for them, I would appreciate seeing my prayers answered before my eyes when I return to see the man in two weeks, and may an overflow of the Spirit's blessings shower upon me so that I will be able to say like Job of old: 'When the ear heard me, then it blessed me; and when the eye saw me, it gave witness to me: because I delivered the poor that cried, and the fatherless, and him that had none to help him. The blessing of him that was ready to perish came upon me' [Job 29:11-13].

"And Father, may this experience bring me closer to my Saviour, 'that I may know him [better], and the power of his resurrection' [Philippians 3:10]. Lord God, as this intercession comes to a close, let it not be the end, but the beginning, of a precious walk with Thee. Again, I thank Thee for Thy love and Thy grace so preciously dispensed in the lives of those I pray for.

"This petition I present in the name of our merciful and faithful High Priest, Christ Jesus, who has acquired the legal right, in the sight of the inhabitants of the galaxies and the angels of heaven, to appropriate to the fallen descendants of Adam His great righteousness and complete salvation."

Candlelight Dinner

Two weeks passed, and with mixed feelings I entered Mr. A's place of business. While I expected to hear of blessings received, it was also possible that the couple could have resisted the leading of the Spirit of God in exercising their God-given right of freedom of choice and have made wrong decisions. But it wasn't long before I realized that things were looking up in their lives.

Stepping into the doorway of the bookkeeper's office, I asked if Mr. A was going to be tied up very long with the man in his office. The bookkeeper stated that I would be able to see him in a few minutes, then invited me to sit down. He added that his boss had just finalized plans to have the shop enlarged. Furthermore, the businessman had been expecting me to stop by that morning. Instantly I lifted up my heart to God in a silent melody of praise as I began to see that the power of His love had been benefiting those I had prayed for.

Mr. A greeted me with a firm handshake and a peaceful expression reflecting God's love. "I have a lot of good news to tell you. Things that are almost unbelievable have taken place since you were here. My wife and I are on good terms again, and life has taken on a new meaning."

As he continued, I could tell that the Spirit of God had been working in their lives. He told me how for three days after I had stopped by his office his wife began acting differently. When he went home for lunch and the evening meal, he found to his surprise the TV turned off and their favorite classical music playing in the background. She was pleasant but seemed lost in her own thoughts. A couple days later she called him at the office and asked if he could work things out so that he wouldn't have to return to the shop after dinner. The man stated that he could, but would probably get home a bit later than usual.

At home she treated him to a candlelight dinner. Then she explained that she had been giving serious thought to the tensions that had threatened their marriage. She now believed herself capable of taking control of her life and stated that she had matured in a few short days from a confused mess to a calm, reasonable person. Furthermore she added that life was too short to waste feeling sorry for oneself when in reality she had so much to be thankful for.

As he described to me what he called his good fortune, my heart thrilled with a joy born of heaven, and silently I thanked and praised the Holy Trinity for making me a channel for God's love and healing.

He then stated how he himself had experienced a few days of self-examination. Both of them had decided to venture on what one could call a new beginning.

"This may be hard for you to believe, but I am telling you without exaggeration that the whole atmosphere of our home has changed," he concluded. "I don't know how to explain it. It's so peaceful, so enjoyable. Coming home is a pleasant experience again."

Now he was making new plans for the business. He

figured that if he were to enlarge the building some and get two additional auto body repairmen, the added revenues would enable him to hire a qualified person to make repair estimates and manage the place. Then he would be able to take some time off every so often, and spend it with his wife.

"How do you explain something so fantastic taking place in so short a time?" he suddenly asked.

Silently, I prayed, "Heavenly Father, please bless my mind with the right thing to say."

Aloud I said, "Mr. A, if you recall, as I left here two weeks ago, I mentioned that I would remember you and your wife in my prayers. Well, what you have experienced is the result of answered prayers."

Shaking his head, he replied, "I believe you, and appreciate greatly your having prayed for us, but I have never seen prayers answered with such power. The Mrs. and I are churchgoing people, but I must admit that I have never seen prayers answered this way—prayers that actually change lives."

To my surprise, his expression and voice suddenly slipped into a note of desperation. "Please, please promise me that you will continue praying for us, please!"

Never in my life had I felt so needed by someone, and at the same time so glad that I was seeing my prayers answered.

"Mr. A, I promise to pray for you and your wife. In fact, I will place your names on my perpetual prayer list. I will see to it that daily intercessions will ascend to God in your behalf."

With the pressure of my schedule in mind, I quickly revised his ad, then left for my next call. I did not work that telephone directory the following year, as I had graduated to major markets, but I met at a regional meeting the fellow who had handled the account, and received some good news.

"Roger, Mr. A sends you his regards. He wanted me

to tell you about the success of his business, and above all, that everything is well with the family. In fact, he said that things have never been better at home. He didn't tell me what you men talked about, but somehow you have made a profound impression upon the man."

It was indeed good news to hear that the Spirit of God was giving intensive care to the couple on a daily basis.

PRAYERS WITH HIGH DIVIDENDS

For many years I had meditated upon the experience of the apostle Paul. It amazed me that Jesus had appeared to the man on his way to Damascus to point out that his religious zeal was misguided.

Think of it—the Lord of glory talking to a man who hurled believers into prison, was instrumental in having many put to death, and even found pleasure in trying to force some of them to blaspheme (Acts 26:10, 11).

Questions kept running through my mind. Why would God follow such a course with Saul of Tarsus? Was He showing favoritism toward Saul by working for his salvation in a manner different from what He was willing to do to save other men into His eternal kingdom?

Then one day as I was sitting in my car waiting in a long line in front of a car wash, an answer came loud and clear. I had my Bible open, reading 1 Timothy 2: "I exhort therefore, that, first of all, supplications, prayers, intercessions, and giving of thanks, be made for all men;

for kings, and for all that are in authority. . . . For this is good and acceptable in the sight of God our Saviour; who will have all men to be saved, and to come unto the knowledge of the truth." I became deeply impressed with the thought that God was calling me to do a work that not even the angels of heaven could do. He wanted me to be an intercessor for the unsaved and the ungodly that I met in my work. And I knew exactly where to find the power to help such people—in prayer and supplication to God, who waits for our requests for help so that He will then have the legal right in the sight of the inhabitants of the universe to move with power into Satan's domain and rescue his captives.

It was while I was working with the telephone directory that I saw God's Holy Spirit work in wonderful ways. But before recounting some of my prayer experiences, I feel it's important to consider the frame of mind that motivated Jesus as He prayed for human beings.

As I have read the Bible through the years, I have observed that our Lord tried constantly to impress the minds of His disciples with His divine compassionate love for fallen mortals. He spent much time in prayer, giving them an example to follow so that they also could become mighty intercessors for others.

When He ascended to heaven He had no fear that His disciples would fail Him as they worked for the salvation of others. He would send them the One who would teach them how to live in such a way as not to fail their Redeemer.

I have found nine essential factors behind successful, victorious, Christian living. When through the Holy Spirit we possess them, we can then ask God that the same blessings may crown the lives of those we pray for. Let's consider those factors closely.

Factor 1

While human love is wrapped up in selfishness and

produces results that are at best shaky and short-lived, *divine compassionate love* is a force that never fails. I find great comfort in the fact that the "Father of infinite pity" so loved humanity that "he gave his only begotten Son, that whosoever believeth in him should not perish, but have everlasting life." We need to hunger and thirst for God to impart that divine force to us.

It is my firm conviction that the reason that Christian homes are breaking up as they are today, devastating the lives of men, women, and children, is that our Christian hearts lack that divine compassionate love. We may not admit it, but the results are speaking louder than words.

Factor 2

The next factor is often greatly misunderstood because of a powerful counterfeit. That valuable element is *heavenly joy*.

Through the ages Satan has misled humans by causing them to believe that they will find joy in self-pleasing and self-serving. And that they can obtain it without consideration for others. But such a lifestyle leads only to disappointment and often great unhappiness.

On the other hand, we will find a joy that never fails in Christ. Romans 15:3 says that "Christ pleased not himself." He found great joy in blessing the lives of others.

About the early disciples the Bible declares, "And the disciples were filled with joy, and with the Holy Ghost" (Acts 13:52).

I believe that today we need to pray for heavenly joy with great intensity and desire. Only then can we work to pass the same blessing to others.

Factor 3

Both the rich and the poor and the strong and the weak seek peace. Because there are various degrees of peace, I like to reach out for the very best—that is, *heav-*

enly peace. That kind of peace brings pleasant relaxation by imparting a mental or spiritual state of mind that frees us from disquieting and perturbing fears.

We think of Jesus, who slept in a boat during a storm (Mark 4:38-40), or of Peter, who slept soundly during the night before his scheduled execution (Acts 12:6).

We today need that same freedom from fear. How can a person acquire such a state of mind? When the Comforter, the Holy Spirit, the representative of Christ on earth, imparts heavenly peace to someone, He completely delivers that person's mind from any fears that would make him or her anxious or restless.

Factor 4

To appreciate this factor, one has to remember the cruel world that we live in. Distresses and perplexities come in many forms, but the most difficult ones are the injustices and unkindness inflicted upon us by others. Sometimes it amounts to harsh and even cruel treatment by individuals who have no control of their tongues.

The apostle James in chapter 3 of his Epistle compares the human tongue to a little fire that turns into an inferno doing vast damage. To survive such experiences one has to receive special help in the form of *longsuffering*, another divine attribute of our Redeemer. When God met with Moses on Mount Sinai, He declared Himself to be "the Lord God, merciful and gracious, longsuffering, and abundant in goodness and truth" (Exodus 34:6).

If we seek a fresh baptism of this heavenly grace on a daily basis, we will be able to put up with the shortcomings of others, and sincerely pray for a divine blessing on their lives also. Then like the apostle Paul we will be able to say, "I can do all things through Christ which strengtheneth me" (Philippians 4:13).

Factor 5

Here we have an element of great value to those engaged in the field of communication. Be it in the business world or in working directly with people who need help, a most valuable asset is *gentleness*.

I was working on the Buffalo, New York, telephone directory for the third year, and the canvass had begun but a few days before. One morning my sales manager told me to come into his office before going out on my calls. Naturally I wondered what was so important that he wouldn't talk about it at my desk.

As I entered his office he asked me to close the door, then phoned the receptionist to say that he would not take any calls until he told her. My heart sank into my chest, since I knew whenever he did that, it spelled trouble. But I regained my composure when he said that he would like me to do him a favor. The conversation went something like this.

"Roger, I have here the files of a large account that needs very special care, and that should be handled by someone who is tactful and at the same time has the patience of an angel, or close to it. This ticket adds up to several hundreds of dollars in monthly billing. As we managers were setting up the assignments for the 43 of you, this account received a lot of discussion as to who was best suited to handle it. We need someone with the finesse, the tact, the expertise to make a favorable impression on the client. Roger, I believe that you are the right man for the job."

"What about the person who had it last year?"

"We cannot let him handle it again, seeing that he had a very difficult time with it. The account was closed 10 days before the book was shipped to the printers, with a loss of almost $200 per month in billing. Our man says that the president of the corporation is most difficult to talk to. He just will not set up an appointment to go over his yellow pages advertising program. Instead he told the rep to drop in two or three times a week until he finds him with some time to spare. The fellow claims that he went there more than 50 times over a period of six months."

As I sized up the situation, I felt extremely reluctant to accept the challenge, then silently prayed, "Jesus, what should I do?" Instantly I knew that the Lord would be with me. I felt that it could turn out to be an occasion for all the managers, and the whole sales force, to see that the Lord God does take care of His people.

My boss reminded me of some difficult business calls he had made with me as an observer in the past, and how impressed he had been of the way I had handled them.

"Roger, I am aware that a great power accompanies you, and I would like the folks here to be made aware of it also. Will you take the challenge, and make me proud of you?"

"I can see that it will take a miracle from God to make a success of this undertaking, but trusting in His power, I believe all will turn out well. I will accept the assignment."

Within 10 days I had closed the account and increased the billing substantially. After praying that the Lord would give me divine tact and gentleness, I phoned for a five-minute appointment with the man, just to introduce myself, and got it on the spot. The positive first contact led to another interview a few days later, where I showed him some ads I had prepared. On that call he was pleased with the work I had done, and to my great surprise asked if I would be willing to see him at his office at 7:00 a.m. so that we could talk about some of his other businesses and additional advertising. The place would be quiet for him till about 9:00 a.m. I agreed to that.

During that interview, while I prepared the ads, he told me of the terrible problem he and his wife were having with their only son. The young man had been the joy of their lives until he became hooked on drugs and got into trouble with the law. They could hardly stand being disgraced that way. He added that the experience had somehow caused him to become unkind to others, something he found himself unable to change. As we conversed I promised to keep them in my daily prayers, which he thanked me for.

About a month later he called me to have a new product line included in his ads. During the conversation he stated that things were getting better at home, and to keep praying for them. I explained that he would have to sign new copy sheets to authorize the changes in his ads, so we set up an appointment for two days later.

As I was rearranging his ads, he told me of some interesting changes that had taken place involving his son. The boy had decided to change his lifestyle, and had sought his parents' help in the matter. The man's wife no longer needed powerful medications to help her nerves. He could sleep entire nights now, and the feeling of carrying the world on his shoulders had left him.

Then he said something that thrilled me. "My wife and I believe that your praying for us has brought great blessings into our lives. I told her that when you left my office a powerful presence of peace and joy remained with me that whole day."

Factor 6

Again we find an attribute of God, one that might frustrate us at first, since the Bible clearly says that we do not have it. It is the element of *goodness*.

The prophet Jeremiah wrote that the human heart is "deceitful above all things, and desperately wicked" (Jeremiah 17:9). The ancient Hebrews failed God miserably because of their lack of goodness. Their unconsecrated lives led to their ruin.

It is a terrific encouragement to know that the Lord is more than eager to provide us with His goodness, and to enable us to experience successful, victorious, Christian living through the indwelling of His Holy Spirit if only we take the time to daily ask for it.

Factor 7

This factor is so vital to one's Christian experience that in its absence spiritual growth will not take place. In fact, the Bible tells us that without it, one cannot please God. That most important factor is a *living faith*.

"Without faith it is impossible to please him: for he that cometh to God must believe that he is, and that he is a rewarder of them that diligently seek him" (Hebrews 11:6).

A living faith is one that increases our spiritual strength, enabling us to develop an unfaltering trust in our heavenly Father, and in the power of His Holy Spirit. Inspired by the Holy Spirit, faith will flourish only as it is cherished.

When a person prays for it, he or she might as well seek the highest degree of faith available. That is genuine biblical faith. It will impart great belief in God, great trust in Him, and above all, a loyalty to Him that will be *immovable*—the kind that we read about in the eleventh chapter of Hebrews.

Factor 8

In a world that promotes self-esteem and self-exaltation on every side, God's people need as never before a precious heavenly trait that adorns the character of Christ. That valuable factor is the *meekness* of Christ.

To be unpretentious, humble, and submissive to God's will is of great value in God's sight. "Thus saith the high and lofty One that inhabiteth eternity, whose name is Holy; I dwell in the high and holy place, with him also that is of a contrite and humble spirit, to revive the spirit of the humble, and to revive the heart of the contrite ones" (Isaiah 57:15).

Factor 9

What is that special power that we need so greatly? It is *self-control* imparted by the Spirit of God.

An old turn-of-the-century dictionary of mine defines self-control as "the ability to check or regulate, to restrain, and to govern self in all aspects of life." We can possess purity of thought, purity of heart, and purity of life even in this day and age by controlling our thoughts with the power of the Spirit of God blessing our minds. Romans 12:21 tells us to "overcome evil with good." Keeping the mind busy with thoughts that will elevate and ennoble one's character is the formula to success here.

I have found by experience that an excellent way to do that is to work at memorizing God's Holy Word. However, I am not the first person to have discovered that. "Thy word have I hid in mine heart, that I might not sin against thee," the psalmist said.

The Word of God says of man, "As he thinketh in his heart, so is he" (Proverbs 23:7). "Who shall ascend into the hill of the Lord? or who shall stand in his holy place? He that hath clean hands, and a pure heart" (Psalm 24:3, 4).

Victory through Christ—what a majestic experience!

Prayers that will produce high dividends for the kingdom of God are ours to experience and enjoy now.

5
A PERPETUAL PRAYER LIST

It was hay fever time, and having awakened at 4:00 a.m. with a fit of sneezing, I took some medication to alleviate the distress. As I realized that sleep had now escaped me, I asked the Lord to lead my mind into meditation and prayer. Immediately I began thinking about the fierce battle the children of Israel found themselves in when the Amalekites attacked them at Rephidim.

Moses, Aaron, and Hur observed the conflict from the top of a hill. Moses, the praying man that he was, stretched out his arms toward heaven, interceding for his people. The battle went in the Israelites' favor until Moses' hands became heavy and he had to put them down. Then the enemy began to prevail.

As the pattern repeated itself a couple more times, Aaron and Hur realized that they had to hold Moses' hands up toward heaven in order for Israel to be victorious. Taking a large stone, they sat their leader on it, then both of them held up his hands all day long till the sun went down and Israel had won the skirmish.

Thoughts of the incident led me to understand that in interceding for those in need, consistency in prayer is of greater importance than I had previously assumed. I recalled how my prayers for others over the years produced little results until I made myself a prayer list, and brought every person before the Lord daily. It was then that I began to see many of my prayers answered before my eyes.

At that point numerous individuals gained victory over the power of sin as in answer to prayer God pushed back the forces of darkness so that they had a chance to think for themselves.

Daily without fail for almost three years I had brought the case of a young man named Robert before the throne of grace, praying that the Holy Spirit would lead him to repentance and help him to make intelligent decisions for his present life and for eternity.

God does not violate anyone's freedom of choice, however. The Spirit of God does not force people into anything that they do not desire. He only shows them a better way of life, and invites them to experience real joy and peace. The choice is theirs to make under these most favorable conditions.

The thought that the Creator treasures human beings who are struggling with the power of sin and are rescued by the power of love more dearly than the unfallen inhabitants of the galaxies filled my heart with surging concern for others. Feeling a sense of responsibility similar to what a father feels about the well-being of his children, I asked myself, "If I were to die, who would plead for the merits of Christ to be appropriated to those on my prayer list?"

Another question popped into my mind: How could I assure that daily intercessions would be made for those who are now receiving help from the Holy Spirit, lest they once more become perplexed, distressed, and oppressed?

With a sense of helplessness, I told myself, "What I need is some kind of perpetual prayer list." I don't know why I said that, but I did, and the thought stuck in my mind.

As a result, I began telling the Lord about my worry that my intercessions could cease suddenly, leaving others deprived of much-needed help.

For the previous couple days I had been memorizing passages from the seventeenth chapter of the Gospel of John about Jesus' great concern for His disciples. From them I knew that He understood the full extent of my concern for my people's needs.

"And now I am no more in the world, but these are in the world, and I come to thee. Holy Father, keep through thine own name those whom thou hast given me. . . . I pray not that thou shouldest take them out of the world, but that thou shouldest keep them from the evil. . . . Neither pray I for these alone, but for them also which shall believe on me through their word" (John 17:11-20).

Christ's words of intercession, encompassing all Christians to the end of time, led me to respond, "Dear Saviour, please make me a wise intercessor for my fellow humans so that the very best of our Father's blessings may crown their lives, leading them to the City of God."

Having spoken that short request, I waited for an answer. The Lord led me to Exodus 28:29. It declares, "Aaron shall bear the names of the children of Israel in the breastplate of judgment upon his heart, when he goeth in unto the holy place, for a memorial before the Lord continually."

Here was the answer to my human limitations. I would have the Lord engrave the names of the many persons on my prayer list upon the breastplate of His righteousness. Were I to die that day, Jesus, the divine Intercessor, would continue to intercede by the mercy seat for them.

Yes, I indeed have a perpetual prayer list. And although over the decades it has grown to hundreds of individuals, the vastness of their needs has not burdened the Great Intercessor. The apostle Paul confidently wrote, "We have not an high priest which cannot be touched with the feeling of our infirmities; but was in all points tempted like as we are, yet without sin. Let us therefore come boldly unto the throne of grace, that we may obtain mercy, and find grace to help in time of need" (Hebrews 4:15, 16).

No Use for Spiritual Things

During the early seventies, while I was working on the Buffalo, New York, telephone directory, my superiors asked me if I was willing to help out in an emergency. The Plattsburgh, New York, telephone canvass was in progress, and a need had arisen for someone who could handle large business accounts, many of them located in Montreal, Canada. It would involve about a month.

I obliged, and tackled the project with vigor. With the divine power of the Holy Spirit opening the way before me, the undertaking turned out to be a great success. In fact, that year I was one of two men given special recognition in New York State, and honored by being made a member of the Sales Achievement Club for outstanding sales performances in yellow pages advertising.

After having called on business accounts in Montreal all day and driven the 60 miles back to Plattsburgh, I arrived at the office about 7:00 in the evening. I quickly posted on the canvass status board the amount of revenue handled that day, and the net gain in advertising dollars. Just then a fellow by the name of Anthony came in to post his report also. He had had an early evening appointment with a building contractor that had prevented him from eating at his regular time, so we decided to have our evening meal together.

As we were eating, Tony asked a couple questions

about my wife and children. A few minutes later he told about his family life.

Again in this case, I saw the Holy Spirit inviting me to include the man in my prayer ministry. Tony was filled with remorse over an incident that had brought tragedy into the lives of several people. It had resulted in the loss of a successful business built up over many years of hard work, and had caused estrangement from his teenage children, whom he loved very much.

It began at a banking firm's Christmas party. He was conversing with the president of the bank and his secretary when the girl who had brought the latter said that because of a call from home she had to leave earlier than intended. Could the secretary get a ride back with someone else? At that moment Tony offered to help.

During the long drive to her place the secretary did most of the talking, and as he listened, the thought entered his mind that he should try to get a kiss for his trouble. He politely asked if she would object to a friendly Christmas kiss. To his great surprise she stated that it was an excellent idea, adding that she had been hoping for a little romance.

That supposedly innocent Christmas kiss turned out to be his undoing. The woman was also married, but had occasionally flirted with Tony when he visited the bank. The Christmas kiss was followed by a New Year's kiss, and developed into an affair.

After a few months of meeting at various motels, the woman's husband had her followed by a private investigator. Furious, the husband phoned Tony's wife to inform her of what had been going on. She in turn went into a rage that led her to demand a divorce settlement that wiped Tony out financially.

He had to sell his business to meet the legal fees and to satisfy the decision of the courts. He and his girlfriend decided to leave town and go to a big city. After working hard for three years at establishing themselves in what they called "their new lives," an unexpected event shattered all their dreams for the future.

The woman's husband contacted her and pleaded for her to return home for the sake of the children. She jumped at the offer, and left Tony so quickly that it stunned him senseless for days.

He tried to escape from his problems through drink. Now he spent his weekends in an alcoholic haze to escape his guilt.

I asked him if he had ever thought of seeking divine help.

"To be honest with you, Roger, I must say that I have no use for spiritual things. In fact, I have not been in a church since I was married, which was years ago."

A couple more questions revealed his almost total lack of knowledge about God and the Bible and his apparent satisfaction with his ignorance. He believed in God as a creative moving force that animates all forms of life, but refused to accept anything that had to do with a personal God.

Then I did something that shocked him. "Tony, seeing that you initiated this conversation and willingly told me about your problems, I want you to know that from this day on, I will be interceding in prayer for you. In fact, I will place your name on my prayer list, never to be removed. And I believe that the Holy Spirit will lead your feet to the City of God."

For a few seconds he was speechless. "I—I—I have never heard anything like that. I don't know just how to express myself here, but I want you to know that—that I am surprised and moved by your interest. The sincerity and power of your convictions, I must admit, have touched me, giving me a strange new feeling. I thank you for what you said." Then he changed the subject.

Because of our busy schedules, we did not have occasion to talk again except for a few words at the office. At the end of my assignment as I was leaving the office on Friday, he accompanied me to the car.

It was then that he made a statement that helped me understand why my commitment to pray for him had so startled him.

"The reason that I was moved so deeply, and almost lost control of my emotions in the presence of everybody in the restaurant, was because I had heard my grandmother say similar things. When I said that I had never heard words like those, what I meant to say was that I had never heard anything like that since my grandmother died. Before she passed away she said to me, 'Anthony, I believe that my prayers for you will be answered, and that the Spirit of God will lead your feet to the City of God.'"

Nine years passed before I met him again. By that time I had been promoted to division sales manager and was visiting a telephone directory canvass in Pennsylvania. One day at noon a couple of my men and I were looking the menu over in a restaurant when someone to my left said, "Roger Morneau, what brings you to this part of the world?"

When I looked up, there stood Tony with his hand extended in greeting. Now the area manager for a large marketing firm, he was with some of his men also, and they were just leaving. He stated that he would like to talk to me and would return in a few minutes and wait in his car until I finished my meal.

As we sat in the car, the very first thing that he did was remind me of our conversation nine years before in a Plattsburgh, New York, restaurant, and how it had been instrumental in getting him to think about those things that have real value in life. Thanking me several times for praying for him, he explained that he no longer used alcohol, had quit smoking, and above all, had become interested in spiritual matters because of some unusual outworkings of divine providence.

After we parted, all day long I kept thanking and

praising Jesus for having led me to understand more fully the power of His ministration in the Holy of Holies of the heavenly sanctuary. Otherwise I would never have experienced the blessing that was mine to know that I have a perpetual prayer list in His carrying the names of all my people upon His heart.

6
INTERCEDING FOR YOUNG PEOPLE

I would like to tell about Robert, a young man whom the Spirit of God cared for and blessed during the time he had drifted away from God.

It was a sad surprise to learn from one of Robert's former college buddies the almost unbelievable changes that had taken place in the young man's life. In a few short years he had gone from being a God-loving young person to one dedicated to total self-centeredness.

"Robert," his college friend said, "is no longer the sharp young Christian you knew him to be. After college he found employment that brought him material prosperity, and in addition his wife's income placed them on easy street.

"They made friends with some of the people they were working with, which gradually led them into places of entertainment that they had not known before. The wife became fascinated by the music, and before long they were both hooked on rock. They occupied their leisure time with activities that not only separated them from God, but eventually from one another. Whether he left her or she left him, I don't exactly know."

The college friend added, "His brother told me that Robert has $1,000 worth of grass and other powerful stuff in his place. He spends hours smoking grass, and he loves heavy rock. In fact, he has sunk thousands of dollars into a top-notch stereo set to create the impression of being near the stage of a rock concert."

When I expressed my disappointment, the young man replied, "Don't feel bad about him. He knew better than to get himself involved in that type of situation. It's obviously what he wanted, or he would have stayed away from it from the beginning."

Naturally I immediately determined to take Robert's case before our heavenly Father on a daily basis. I prayed that the Holy Spirit would bring Robert victory over rock music, liquor, and drugs. Naturally I realized that it could possibly take years before the man could reach a position where he could make decisions that would lead back to God, but I was prepared to pray for him the rest of my life.

Three years went by; then one day I had a wonderful surprise. I met Robert at a religious meeting. The next day I had the joy of hearing from him how the Spirit of God had worked in his behalf.

"It was about a year ago," he told me, "when I began to experience a change in the way I reasoned regarding my friends, my leisure time, my musical preferences, and other aspects of my daily life. Up to that time I had spurned spiritual things, and for a period of five years had given myself up to enjoying what the world calls the good life.

"From the time that I got up each morning to when I retired at night I was either involved in some form of self-gratification or living in anticipation of it. For instance, the very first thing I did each morning was to play some of my favorite rock music as I got ready for work. There was something about it that satisfied an inner craving.

"Every weekend was taken up with a wild party roaring with women, liquor, grass, and whatever else could liven it up. By then my wife and I had parted ways, and I was completely free to do whatever I wanted. And I loved it that way. But suddenly I came face-to-face with reality."

"Would you mind telling me about it?" I asked.

"About a year ago things began to change. First, my rock music and my beer went flat on me. One evening when I arrived home from work, I turned on the stereo set, placed a stack of favorite records on the turntable, then sat comfortably with a glass of my favorite beer in one hand and a newspaper in the other. I took a couple sips from the glass and read a few minutes, but when I had a third sip, I sensed that something had gone wrong. That mouthful of beer tasted bad. In fact, it was awful.

"I went to the refrigerator for another can, and after opening it, I found that it tasted worse than the first one. And the music was not the same—something was missing. It wasn't enjoyable as it had been, so I checked the controls on the amplifier. They were set correctly, but the rock music had lost a great deal of its appeal, and I could not zero in on that missing element.

"Just then the doorbell rang, and there stood Henry, a close buddy. 'Henry, you came to visit at the right time. Something strange is taking place, and I can't figure it out.' After pouring the rest of the last can of beer into a glass, I handed it to him. Tasting it, Henry pronounced it excellent. I told him that mine tasted less than good.

" 'Let me taste the beer in your glass; I can't believe you.' After taking a mouthful, he headed for the kitchen sink, then sputtered, 'That was putrid. Awful stuff. Man, you have a real problem here, and I can't help you. I don't want to scare you, but I believe that a supernatural force is at work here. By the way, I came to borrow one of your tools for a couple days.'"

My interest in Robert's experience was naturally mounting, and I couldn't help asking him what he thought of his friend's comment about the supernatural.

"My first thought," Robert replied, "was that someone had been praying for me and the Lord was doing something to get me to give some serious thought to my way of life. The experience kind of stunned me, and from that day on I could no longer drink beer."

As we chatted, he gave me additional details about the incident, but I was most impressed by what he described next.

"A couple days after the beer incident, I almost lost my life. It was a November evening about 8:00, and I was driving down a small hill. Since it had been raining and the road surface was beginning to freeze in spots, I had slowed down to about 35 miles per hour when suddenly four deer jumped onto the road. The headlights startled them, and they halted in the middle of the road.

"Instantly I slammed on the brakes, and the car started to spin like a top on a glass table. It kept going in circles without hitting the shoulders of the road, and continued all the way to the bottom of the hill. After the first turn, I saw that the deer had vanished, but there was no way of stopping the car. After a couple hundred feet the road was level again and the car slowed right down and came to rest sideways against a guardrail.

"It was on the driver's side of the car, and after regaining my composure, I looked over the rail with my flashlight and saw a drop of about 80 feet."

When I asked him what thoughts went through his mind when he realized that he was safe, he replied, "I felt impressed that someone's prayers had been answered. Naturally those two experiences started me

thinking very seriously about the fact that someone valued my life more greatly than I did.

"It also encouraged me to return to God when I realized that while I had given up on Him, He had not
abandoned me. From that time on, I found myself
weighing what I was doing in this present life against
the reality of eternal life. I had a lot of backtracking to
do in order to get on the right road again. Drugs had a
powerful hold on me, one that I knew I could not break
myself. But I decided to talk the whole matter over with
Jesus, and to follow as He would lead. And lead He did.
Today I am a free man again, having had victory over
self, over sin, and over the world."

Robert's story strengthened my prayer ministry and
helped me acquire more completely something that I
had been seeking for a long time: an unfaltering trust in
my heavenly Father, and in the power of His Holy Spirit.

Reflections

I don't agree with those Christian parents who as-
sume that if their sons or daughters depart from the
Lord, there isn't much that we or God can do, because
the young people are exercising their freedom of choice.
Such parents believe that all they can do is pray that the
Lord will watch over their wayward children.

Such reasoning can have disastrous results. While it
is true that God will not force the will, yet through our
intercessions that claim the blood of Christ, His Spirit
can overrule the forces of darkness and control events in
such a way that the ones we are praying for will be
helped to decide for right—even if they have to experience some suffering.

Let's consider Samson's experience. I can imagine
how distressed Manoah and his wife must have been
when the boy they had brought up for God began to as-
sociate with idolaters. For 20 years as he ruled Israel he
kept repeating immorality. Then one day Manoah came

from the city and told his wife that he had some real bad news, that she better sit down, as she would be shocked. He stated that the Philistine rulers had put out Samson's eyes while he was visiting a woman in the valley of Sorek.

I am inclined to believe that while Mrs. Manoah felt terrible at hearing the news, she wasn't shocked to the extent of believing that God had failed them. Surely they prayed that God would somehow save Samson in His eternal kingdom, regardless of what it would take to bring their son to his senses.

In prison Samson did some serious thinking. Scene after scene of his childhood days passed before him. He turned to God with his whole heart, and in the eleventh chapter of Hebrews we read that he will stand before God someday with all other champions of faith.

7

PRAYING FOR THOSE WHO DON'T KNOW GOD

I have seen almost unbelievable changes take place in the lives of many through intercession on their behalf. The success I have experienced over the years in my prayer ministry is totally a result of the divine outworking of God's Holy Spirit. I cannot claim any glory to myself.

We are in a fierce conflict with the powers of darkness for the control of human minds. And I have found by experience that God's Holy Spirit alone can bring victory here. Through intercessory prayer I have seen the way open for God to exercise His divine grace toward most undeserving individuals.

As time went by in my work and I returned year after year to review the yellow pages advertising of my customers, and saw how the Spirit of God changed and brightened the lives of some of the ungodly persons I had been praying for, I became more excited about my prayer ministry.

I asked the Lord to lead me into a deeper prayer experience with Him, so that I could see His Spirit bless the lives of a greater number of people. It wasn't long before He answered my prayers.

By now I was in my 50s and had passed up many opportunities to get into management. But one day I concluded that the time had arrived to make a change in my occupation. Physically I was beginning to slow down, and a statement my boss had made a while back echoed in my mind: "Roger, you should give serious thought to earning your living by sharing your experience with younger men, especially when you are reaching the point where nature will no longer allow you to work such long hours."

He reminded me of a number of successful managerial experiences I had had from filling in in emergencies, such as a 1970 assignment to help the New Brunswick telephone company restructure their telephone directory operation for that Canadian province.

After having accepted the responsibility, I had suggested making many of the directories bilingual, since in some areas of the Maritime Provinces the population is 50 to 75 percent Frenchspeaking. After leading the sales force for a number of weeks to get things going in the right direction, I returned to Buffalo, New York.

With the blessing of God the New Brunswick assignment turned out to be a huge success, and from that time on, upper management kept offering me managerial positions that I had declined. If I went into management, I wondered, would it hinder the Lord's blessing? Would I find myself working in my own feeble human strength? If I assumed responsibility of men who at times profaned the name of God by their language, would it affect God's ability to prosper my own work?

Many of the men that would be working under me, though cultured and well-mannered college graduates, would be lacking an experience with God. Isaiah 59:1, 2 had guided my life for many years: "Behold, the Lord's hand is not shortened, that it cannot save; neither his ear heavy, that it cannot hear: but your iniquities have separated between you and your God, and your sins have hid his face from you, that he will not hear." I wanted nothing to come between me and God.

Again and again I kept asking myself, Would the behavior of those under me raise a barrier between me and God so that He could not bless my work? I placed the matter in prayer before the Lord and asked that He would clearly answer my questions and open a clear path for me to follow.

But first I went through a couple experiences that broadened my understanding of how to remove the wall of separation that many have erected to hide the face of God from themselves.

Shocked Into Prayer

One Friday afternoon in April as I drove home from work, I passed a F. W. Woolworth store and decided to stop and pick up a couple items that I needed. Returning to my car, I thought I might as well take a few minutes to process the day's paperwork.

The thermometer had reached into the high 70s. Getting into the car, I quickly opened the windows and let the heat out. A few minutes later a green Mercury pulled into a parking place two spaces away. Glancing out of the corner of one eye, I saw a middle-aged couple with the woman at the steering wheel.

"Mary, you will have to turn the key so that I can roll up this power window," the man said.

"Jim, you're stupid. I've told you a hundred times to roll the windows up while the engine is still running. Won't you ever learn?"

The man opened his mouth, and a flurry of profanities poured out, a mixture of the sacred and profane such as could not fail to get the message across to his wife that her words had touched a sensitive spot. Getting angrier by the moment, he accused her of having wrecked what had been a perfect day by refusing to keep her big mouth shut.

What a wicked man, I thought to myself. Then I immediately prayed, "Jesus, please forgive them. By the mighty power of Thy Holy Spirit, please rebuke the demonic forces oppressing their minds, and bless their lives with the sweet peace of Thy love."

Instantly the verbal storm stopped. For about 20 seconds neither said a word, then the man broke the silence. "Mary, I am sorry I got so angry. Really, I feel bad now that I spoke to you in the way I did. I don't know why I get so angry at times. I can actually feel anger swell up in me toward people I dearly love. Please forgive me, and I promise to put forth real effort not to repeat these outbursts."

Then it was beautiful to hear her admit that she was at least partly at fault for not being careful with her words, and at times actually took pleasure in verbally jabbing him. Promising to be more considerate in the future, she gave him a peck of a kiss, put the window up, and they both got out of the car to go shopping.

Stepping to the parking meter, the husband studied his coins to feed the meter, and having no dime or nickels, turned to his wife. "Sugar pie, would you be kind enough to look in your purse for a dime?"

"How can I refuse to help when you are treating me as a lady? Do you realize, Jim, that you haven't called me your sugar pie since the kids were little?" After he put the coins in the meter, she grabbed him by the arm, and like two newlyweds they proceeded to do some shopping.

As I sat in my car I was more than surprised over the drastic transformation that had taken place in their lives, and at the same time a new dimension had been added to my Christian experience. Never before had I asked the Lord to forgive someone. Only a sense of shock had impelled me to pray for them. When the verbal abuses started to fly, I realized that the man probably hadn't asked for his sins to be forgiven in many years. Knowing that sin separates between God and man, I sensed the urgency of the moment and asked the Lord to give both of them special help.

It amazed me to see how quickly and how differently the couple's outlook changed when the Spirit of God touched their lives. And I had been instrumental in opening the way by my intercession. The thought that during His ministry on earth Jesus carried out that kind of problem-solving now deeply impressed me.

To the paralytic who was hoping for physical healing, Jesus said, "Thy sins are forgiven thee" (Luke 5:20). First the Lord removed from the helpless man his burden of sin, then He did the next best thing, that is, healed his infirmity. At Simon's house, when a woman seeking peace for her soul anointed the Saviour's feet with expensive ointment, Jesus said, "Thy sins are forgiven. . . . Thy faith hath saved thee; go in peace" (Luke 7:48-50).

That's it, I said to myself. *My first concern in praying for the ungodly and the wicked is to ask Jesus to deal with their burdens of sin.* My heart rejoiced in the fact that my Lord is an expert in salvation, specializing in hopeless cases. As I was driving home, my heart filled with thanksgiving over His infinite goodness and grace.

I prayed that if it were pleasing in His sight I would like to have another similar experience, one that would again demonstrate the power of the Holy Spirit to bless once the burden of sin has been removed.

In a Bad Mood

The manager of a large lumber and building supply operation told me that it would be difficult to talk to the owner about his advertising because he owned other businesses that took him out of town a lot. The directory canvass supervisor had given me the account to handle, with the understanding that if I could not see the owner on the premises during canvass time, I could close it over the phone at a later date. After all, the man hadn't changed his advertising program for years. Besides, he had previously refused to make appointments, and seemed to run his businesses according to the way he felt on a particular day.

Because I passed in front of his place of business every day, I stopped every so often. But it was not until Monday of my last week in the area that the manager informed me that the owner desired additional advertising, and wanted to change some of the copy in his existing ads. The boss was in, but in a bad mood. "Too many things to attend to," the manager said. I asked him to get me a definite appointment to see the owner, or he would find himself having the same program in the coming telephone directory. A message left at the telephone office that afternoon indicated that the owner would see me Wednesday at 10:00 a.m.

Wednesday was a beautiful day, and up to that time all had gone well. Entering the establishment, I found it to be a beehive of activities. Spotting the manager from a distance, I made my way to the counter, where he was serving a customer. He told a clerk to finish serving his client, and we walked up to the second floor and the owner's office.

Along the way he mentioned that it was unfortunate that I had to see the boss on this day. The man was in a really bad mood. To begin with, he had arrived with a somber expression. "Must have gotten up on the wrong side of the bed." A short while later he exploded when told that a shipment he had been promised for that day had been delayed through unexpected circumstances. "So prepare yourself for anything," the manager warned. "If the boss shouts at you, don't pay attention to him. It's probably the price he has to pay for being wealthy."

Arriving at the glassed-in office, the manager opened the door and announced me.

"Have him come in and sit down," the owner replied. "I can't talk to him right now, as I have to make a phone call."

As I entered, he didn't even look at me, but kept shuffling papers on his desk. *What a rude person he is,* I thought for a moment. Then I realized that the man was under terrible pressures. His expression reflected internal turmoil. He was undoubtedly a chain smoker, as the office was full of smoke and the ashtray with cigarette butts, and he had a cigarette between his fingers.

After dialing a number on the phone, he began talking to one of his managers in a way I wouldn't have thought possible. Only a tyrant would have used the abusive language that he blasted the man's ears with. He was unhappy about the figures shown on the quarterly report of one of his businesses. Profanities flew right and left, and the more he talked, the more brutal he seemed to get.

This fellow is disgusting—he makes me want to vomit, I thought to myself. Then the memory of my prayer a few days before struck me. Here indeed was another opportunity to pray for an ungodly person so that I could see God remove the individual's burden of sin and the Holy Spirit move with power to help that person "in the battle against principalities and powers, the rulers of the darkness of this world, and wicked spirits in high places."

Unfortunately, I had no desire to pray for him. Yes, I knew that it was the right thing to do, and I made a special effort to pray. "Dear Jesus, I need Your help. I just don't feel like praying for this wicked man. In fact, I would like to walk out of here. You have instructed us to love the unlovable, and for that reason I pray for special help now.

"Please help me to see this man not as he is now, but as he will be by Your grace on that great day when You will resurrect and translate the people of Your righteousness."

Immediately a sense of pity for the man filled my heart, and I continued to pray. "Break through, I pray, the gigantic wall of separation that he has erected to hide himself from Thy face, thereby depriving himself of the sweet peace of our heavenly Father's love and grace.

"Lord, through the power of Thy Holy Spirit, please rebuke the demonic forces that may have been oppressing this man's mind, driving him to sow misery in the lives of others. And having done this, please surround him with a divine atmosphere of light and peace as Thy Spirit abides with him this day, speaking to his heart of the ways of righteousness. Thank You, Lord, for always hearing my petitions for help to the needy."

I determined there and then that this man was going to be in my daily prayers. Immediately I felt the powerful presence of the Spirit of God. I should mention here that my Christian experience has never been dependent upon my feelings, but upon a "Thus saith the Lord." At times when the going has been rough I have been tempted to believe that God has left me to carry my burden alone, but in the end I come to see how graciously the Spirit of God is watching over me. However, there have been a number of occasions when our heavenly Father especially honored me by manifesting His presence in an unmistakable way.

A Transformed Man

It wasn't more than five seconds before I witnessed a transformation in the man as great as night and day. His conversation took on a new sense of direction. Instead of talking almost continually and shouting profanities, he softened the tone of his voice and began to speak with what appeared to be intelligent reasoning. Long pauses gave the other person a chance to explain the situation. The conversation closed on what appeared to be a tensionless note, and he hung up the phone. His stern expression that had at first appeared as unchangeable as some of those seen on monuments in city parks now softened.

A smile took form as he turned toward me. "I am Dennis D," and he stood up behind his desk to extend his hand toward me in a friendly way.

"Roger Morneau here," I said as I firmly shook his hand.

"It's nice meeting you, Roger. It's too bad that you happened to come on a day when everything is running rough."

Then he corrected himself. "I shouldn't be giving you the impression that the conversation you have just witnessed is a rare occurrence. To be honest with you, I must admit that I am—I am at times a madman. I am not crazy or deranged in any way, but there is something strange here. I can't understand why I get so steamed up at times over things that no one has any power to change. And such incidents seem to be more frequent and powerful as time passes. Too often I feel an uncontrollable anger building up within, and I lash out at everybody."

I could tell that the man was deeply distressed by his situation. "If it weren't for the fact that I pay my managers twice as much as they are worth, none of them would work for me." Suddenly he realized that he was talking to a complete stranger. "What am I doing, telling you the secrets of my life? Please excuse me for dumping my problems on you. Let's talk advertising."

"Mr. D, please relax, and trust me," I said. "The very first requirement of my job is to keep in strict confidence whatever my advertisers tell me, and I have successfully done that for years. Quite frequently people tell me things they have told no one else, stating that they feel comfortable in my presence, and believe that it is better to open one's heart to a stranger than to someone who knows them well."

His reply surprised me some, as it was totally unexpected. "Roger, I agree with what your customers say. I can feel a power accompanying you that I don't know exactly how to explain, except to say that it is out of this world. I have never before experienced the peace and quiet that I do now."

"Thank you, sir, for telling me that. Mr. D, I feel that it is important for me to add that from the moment you began talking over the phone, I turned my heart in prayer to the great Monarch of the galaxies, the Lifegiver, asking that He would bless your life with the presence of His Spirit that alone can bring peace and help to those in this world."

He studied me for a moment, then said, "I gave up on religion and God a long time ago. But today you have given me something to think about: the Monarch of the galaxies and His power to touch people's lives in a meaningful way. I like that thought. Don't get me wrong. I am not thinking of going to church or anything like that, but would you be kind enough to keep me in your prayers? I sure would appreciate that."

After I assured him that I would be honored to add his name to my prayer list, we then updated his advertising program. As I got up to leave, he said, "Let me walk down with you, as I have to go downstairs anyway."

On the way, I asked him how he had built such a fine business operation. His face lit up, and he told stories all the way to the front door. Shaking my hand as we parted, he asked if I would be kind enough to see him at the beginning of the telephone directory canvass the following year.

I did not work the directory that year, but I found myself visiting the area two years later as division sales manager, and went on that call with the fellow who had the account. The man was delighted to see me again and was very courteous, and while a new ad was being set up, he had me walk with him to another office to meet his accountant.

After introducing us, he stated that I was the person who had given him a new lease on life, and at the same time saved him a bundle of money, as he no longer had any need "to see his shrink."

A great transformation had taken place in that individual's life. He was vibrant with the joy of living. On the wall in back of his desk hung a lovely plaque with "Prayer changes things" inscribed on it.

Indeed it does—and in this particular instance, I am inclined to believe that of all the blessings received, I was the greater beneficiary of the two of us. That prayer experience had straightened out my warped reasoning that for a number of years had kept me from asking for special help for the ungodly. But from that time on, the Lord was able to use me to open the way so that His Spirit could then move in a marvelous manner to benefit the lives of many others.

8

EVERY PROBLEM A CALL TO PRAYER

As division sales manager of the Northeast Division, covering a geographical area of eight states, I spent most of my time visiting telephone directory canvasses in progress.

Looking over several weekly sales reports, I decided to visit our yellow pages salespeople working on a major directory in Pennsylvania. One man's sales results in particular had caught my attention. Previously a top achiever, he was now experiencing a substantial loss of revenue. I concluded that Charles had a problem that interfered with his work.

Conversing with him, I found that his ex-wife, who had custody of their two children, was making it difficult for him to see their children. In addition, his ex-mother-in-law was doing everything possible to turn the children against him, which just about broke his heart. He admitted that he had a hard time keeping his mind on his work, and that if things didn't improve soon, he would have to quit his job.

I asked for the mother-in-law's name so that I could pray for her. He was a bit surprised by my request, but gave it after commenting that "I doubt that prayers will help, seeing that my parents have been praying for the old witch from the day I married her daughter. In fact, they even had a couple of Masses celebrated so that she would not break up our home, and that didn't help." To make a long story short, I placed the names of the ex-wife, ex-mother-in-law, and the kids on my prayer list along with that of Charles, and every morning, with my Bible open at the twenty-seventh chapter of Matthew, I interceded in their behalf. And above all I prayed that the Spirit of God would help Charles carry his burdens without falling apart.

It was company procedure that all yellow pages representatives would phone the division office in Virginia on Friday between 1:00 and 3:00 in the afternoon to report their figures for the week completed. They stated the amount of advertising dollars handled, the decrease or loss, the net figure, and any changes in number of advertisers.

As I traveled home on Friday, I would stop after 3:00 and phone the office to get the sales results of the men that needed my close attention. It was extremely encouraging, and at the same time a blessing to my Christian experience, to get Charles's figures and see how the Spirit of God was blessing, guiding, directing, and encouraging him as those sales results improved from week to week.

Sometime later I heard all about it from the man himself. With a joy born of heaven, he told how things were changing for the better. He said a couple times, "Your prayers have real power. They really work for people."

While company policies prevented me from talking religion with my people, I was able to live my religious convictions, and I thank God for that. I was surprised to hear one of their comments about living my religion. Because of a health problem, a rep's doctor told him that he had to move to a warm climate. Before leaving for California, he came to see my wife and me. To my great surprise, he told Hilda in my presence about the high regard my associates had for me. "One fellow stated that the day he begins going to church again, he will go to Roger's church. He will belong to a church that has power."

A Liquor Problem Solved

George was a good worker, but on weekends he usually rewarded himself for a job well done by drinking. A single man, he lived in Boston, but one weekend had stayed in a New England city where he was working on the telephone directory. On Friday evening he drank too much and somehow landed in jail. He called the manager of the telephone company, who bailed him out. The next morning after having sobered up, he figured that he should not delay in trying to save his job.

He thought of calling me, but assumed that I, a religious person, would likely fire him on the spot. Instead he called the division office in Virginia with the hope that he might be able to talk to my boss, whom he presumed would be more compassionate, since the man was a social drinker. My superior told George that I made those kinds of decisions, and that I would be at the telephone office on Monday to discuss the matter with him.

On Sunday evening my boss phoned me at home, told about the problem, and suggested that on Monday I call a meeting of our people working the directory and, in the presence of everyone, fire the man.

Having prayed about the matter, I decided against such a move, and talked to George in private. As I traveled to the office I prayed for wisdom to handle the situation with tact. In fact, I felt that maybe I should keep him in our employ, and use his problem for a prayer experience. I believed that the Spirit of God would give the man victory over his drinking by my interceding for him. That is, if the Spirit of God would first cause him to plead with sincerity for his job.

Then I thought, *George is too proud a man to humble himself to the point of pleading for his job. He'll turn in the company materials and quit before he does that.*

However, I found the man highly distressed over his problem. As I listened to his request for compassion, I realized that he was fighting a real battle against liquor.

It was with tears in his eyes that he finally said, "Please give me another chance! Please!"

"George," I replied, "another chance I am giving you. But seeing that I am sticking my neck out for you, I am going to help you in giving up liquor by praying that God will bless your life and give you victory over your drinking."

Thanking me, he said, "However, I don't think that prayers will help. My mother has been praying for 15 years over my problem. She has recited the rosary and paid to have Masses celebrated so that I would get victory over the problem, but it has not helped."

"Well, George, I believe in miracles, so let's see what will happen."

That's exactly what did take place—a miracle brought about by God's Holy Spirit. A few months later he told me how delighted he was that he had given up drinking. He had lost all sense of pleasure from his drinking.

I wish to again make a point very clear: while the Holy Spirit doesn't force a person's will, He can do a lot to change a person's course of action in answer to persevering supplications to God in faith.

Putting on the Brakes

After attending a managers' meeting at the home office in Kansas City, I returned to the Northeast Division with a new objective in mind: to reduce the high turnover of yellow pages advertising salespeople in our division.

At the airport as we waited for my flight to take off, I conversed with two other division sales managers about the concept. They felt that for the vice president of sales to attempt such a thing was ridiculous. It would mean making all our people top producers, they said, and that couldn't be done. Many reps had problems at home that forced them to quit their work. Others, though well-intentioned and hard workers, just didn't have what it took to be successful. So there was only one thing to do, they argued—keep putting new people through training school, costly though that might be. There was no other way.

As for myself, I already knew that with the Holy Spirit blessing my people and their advertising customers, remarkable improvements could be made. Charles's experience along with George's had already proved that.

Some time went by, and on a Thursday evening my boss called me from Kansas. I had been at the Holiday Inn in Lowell, Massachusetts, for three days interviewing sales applicants referred to us by the Snelling and Snelling Employment Agency. "How many men will you have in next month's training class in Kansas City?" he immediately asked.

"As things now stand," I replied, "there will be no one attending."

After a long pause, he inquired, "Aren't you going to replace the three fellows who are trailing at the back of the sales force, the new fellows you and I talked about last week?"

"At the time of our conversation I was leaning in that direction, but today I am thinking differently. Boss, please excuse the analogy, but I have come to the conclusion that this business of letting people go after they have been with us for five months simply because they have not produced great results is a bit ridiculous. It's like acquiring thoroughbreds, casting them aside if they don't win a major race in the first year, and then turning around and buying more of the same.

"Believe me, sir, none of the people I have been talking to this week have impressed me as being better than the fellows we now have. If it's OK with you, I would like to keep the three, spend some time with them in the field, and try to make our present investments pay off."

"I am delighted to hear you talk that way. You know that I am progress-minded."

"If you recall, at our last managers' meeting the vice president of sales stated that it costs our company about $5,000 to have a man in school for a month and in the field for five months. What I would like to do—if it meets with your approval—is to try saving some of that $5,000. What do you say?"

"I don't understand exactly how you are going to make top producers out of those three, but I sure would like to see you try. I am with you 100 percent, but I must tell you that if you proceed that way, you are going to step on the toes of the national sales manager, and you may make yourself an enemy. He has established a top-notch training school on the premise that a lot of high-caliber people going through its doors are needed to obtain a large percentage of top producers."

"I can't see why he would be unhappy with the vice president of sales encouraging us to try reducing the high turnover."

"He shouldn't, but he will if you are successful, because you will have started a trend that will jeopardize the future of his school."

"I appreciate your telling me about this," I said, "but I will not let it change my plans."

"Now we have another problem. He is expecting to have 35 men in the coming class. I have already notified him of our plans to have three recruits attending. But tomorrow morning I will tell him of your decision. Prepare yourself for a telephone call from Roy before the day is over." I had placed my plans before the Lord and felt impressed that I was going in the right direction, and determined to let no one change my mind. But you can rest assured that I spent a lot of time praying for those fellows. The next three weeks I spent with them in the field, one week for each man. I went with them on all their business calls, and to pleasantly surprise them, during the first two days I handled all calls myself.

I placed them into such a relaxed state of mind that they found the experience a real pleasure. We chatted about a great many things, enabling me to learn much about their homes, the members of their families, etc. The men felt that they had benefited highly from the experience, which served to encourage them and produced good sales results. I believe that the Spirit of God had led me in that direction so that I could have the privilege of bringing the rich blessings of God into their homes through my intercessory prayers.

My prayer list grew longer and longer as I got to know my people better. And the time came when I didn't even turn the radio on in my car for the news, but spent all my traveling time interceding in prayer for someone. I should add that of the five divisions of Continental Telephone, the Northeast Division became known as the division with the lowest turnover of yellow pages representatives in the entire nation.

My boss often told the higher-ups that I was the man that had the power to put the brakes on and bring the turnover of our sales force in the Northeast Division to a solid stop. While he gave me the recognition, he knew that the power came from above. I made doubly sure that he understood that.

At the time that I was made district sales manager the Northeast Division was the least productive of all the divisions. But because of the blessings of God, in a few short years we reached the top. In 1977 my boss and I were awarded the Masters Circle Award for our division's coming in first place for that year, excelling in all phases of company operations.

From then on to the time that I left the company in 1981, our division had the lowest turnover of salespeople and stood at the top in all other company objectives except for net increase to advertisers. (The Pacific Division, because of the phenomenal prosperity of the state of California, held that honor.)

9

A FLOOD OF HEALING GRACE

It is a medical miracle that I am still alive today.

My most recent brush with death began one Saturday night as I prepared to retire for the evening about 10:30 p.m. Going to the bathroom, I suddenly found myself passing blood. Instantly I called my wife, Hilda. Although surprised at the sight of all that blood, she is a nurse and managed to remain calm. Opening a closet door, she grabbed a disposable diaper from a box that we kept on hand for our little granddaughter. Then she rushed me to the emergency room of one of the three hospitals of the Triple Cities area of southern New York.

Because I am on a blood thinner as a result of a heart condition, the emergency room physician was not able to stop the bleeding until 2:00 Sunday morning. Then I had to wait until the results from my lab work came back.

An orderly escorted me back from the lab to a small room. Pointing to a high, wheeled table, he said, "Please

wait here, and the doctor will be with you shortly."
About 15 minutes later the orderly returned and found
me still standing there. "Oh! Mr. Morneau, you should
be sitting down. Please wait, and I'll be right back."
Seconds later he brought a footstool about 10 inches in
height, placed it by my feet, and hurried out.

"That's an awfully small thing to sit on," I said to
myself, "but it beats standing up." Making myself as
comfortable on it as possible, I sat with my back against
the frame of the table and my feet stretched out horizon-
tally. Another 15 minutes passed. Then a nurse appeared holding a syringe with a long needle. "Hi! How
are you doing down there?" she said, looking at me.
"Sir, you should have used the footstool to step up and
sit on the table."

Realizing how foolish I must have looked, I burst
out laughing. The nurse gave me the injection, then de-
parted with a smile, probably unable to wait to tell her
colleagues about her befuddled patient.

A week later I received a phone call from a specialist
in urology named Dr. Wise. He had gone over my test results and asked me to see him in his office the next day.

When I arrived at his office, he told me with the ut-
most tact and concern that I had cancer of the prostate.
A large tumor had been the cause of my great loss of
blood. The cancer had progressed beyond the point
where it could be treated with chemotherapy. The only
option left was surgery. After discussing my heart condition, he said he would consult with Dr. Smart, my cardiologist, about the risks of me undergoing surgery.

As I have mentioned earlier, I had almost died in the
intensive care unit of the Greater Niagara General
Hospital back in December of 1984. Tests later revealed
that a virus had destroyed a large part of my heart,
leaving me disabled with cardiomyopathy, a disease of
the heart muscle. Dr. Smart then told my wife that he
did not expect me to live longer than a few months, a

fact that I did not learn until about a year ago.

In such cases the heart usually disintegrates until it kills the patient. In my case the heart tissue instead turned into a hard substance that I can compare only to leather. But with 60 percent of my heart destroyed and my blood constantly thinned to prevent clotting, I was a very poor candidate for any kind of surgery.

About 9:00 that evening the phone rang. To my surprise, it was Dr. Smart. He told me that he had spoken to the urologist about my having surgery and wanted to make sure that I understood the great risk I would be taking with my heart in such a weak condition. In fact, he believed that it was possible that I might not make it through the operation.

Hilda and I had a long conversation about what we should do; then we prayed for God to help us make an intelligent decision. That night I didn't sleep much as I considered my possible death. Yet as I looked back over my life I felt comforted by how the Lord had repeatedly intervened through the years.

Constantly God had wiped away tears, soothed pain, removed anxiety, dispelled fear, supplied wants, and bestowed unending blessings. As I thought about what He had already done in my life, my faith strengthened, and I asked myself, "Why am I thinking about dying when I serve the living God, the Lord of glory in whom dwelled 'the Spirit of life' [Romans 8:2]?"

Verses of Scripture began to fill my mind. "Like as a father pitieth his children, so the Lord pitieth them that fear him. For he knoweth our frame; he remembereth that we are dust" (Psalm 103:13, 14). "By him were all things created, that are in heaven, and that are in earth, visible and invisible, whether they be thrones, or dominions, or principalities, or powers: all things were created by him, and for him: And he is before all things, and by him all things consist" (Colossians 1:16, 17). "For in him dwelleth all the fullness of the Godhead bodily.

And ye are complete in him, which is the head of all principality and power" (Colossians 2:9, 10).

Then my heart thrilled with a joy born of heaven as I considered Matthew 4:23, 24: "And Jesus went about all Galilee, teaching in their synagogues, and preaching the gospel of the kingdom, and healing all manner of sickness and all manner of disease among the people. And his fame went throughout all Syria: and they brought unto him all sick people that were taken with divers diseases and torments, and those which were possessed with devils, and those which were lunatick, and those that had the palsy; and he healed them."

Encouraged and comforted, I began to pray.

"Precious Jesus, You are my strength and my Redeemer. As I look to the Holy of Holies of the heavenly sanctuary where You are ministering in behalf of fallen humanity, I thank You for leaving the courts of glory to come to this land of the enemy. Your blood, shed on the cross, has washed away all my iniquities and my sins, the errors of my ways, and the evil of my fallen human heart. And for all the mercies of Thy love, and the blessings of Thy grace, I thank Thee, Lord, from the bottom of my heart.

"As You are well aware, my human capacities are at a low ebb. Death and 'him that had the power of death, that is, the devil' [Hebrews 2:14] approach to carry me to the grave. But I refuse to believe that it is my time for death.

"Five years ago You delivered me from death in the hospital. At that time You led me into a special prayer ministry, and I have seen You bless great numbers of people in response to my intercessions on their behalf. I do not believe that You want this work of mine to close at this time.

"You know, Lord, that I am not afraid to die. It is just that I enjoy praying for others so very much, and I see myself as a door opener. One who rushes from prison to prison asking You to release spiritual captives bound in shackles of sin.

"Now, Lord, I am not trying to tell You what to do or how to do it. But as I see it, in 10 days I am scheduled to have surgery. If it is Your will, let Your great power of life permeate my being so that when the surgeon operates he will find no tumor or cancer present.

"Lord, I have so many individuals to pray for that I feel that I must not waste my time praying for myself. I will not speak again of my own physical needs. Instead my prayer is only 'May Thy will be done in my life, to the glory of the Father, Son, and Holy Spirit.'"

And with that prayer I rested in His love and grace.

On the day of my surgery the orderlies wheeled me into an operating room equipped with the most up-to-date surgical apparatus. Everything shone with a brilliance that spoke of cleanliness and care.

Five hours later I found myself back in my room and feeling fine. Sometime later Dr. Wise came in to see how I was doing. He informed me that he had not found any trace of a tumor. Also, he seemed surprised when I told him that I felt no pain. The patient in the bed next to me had had the same kind of surgery, and he needed injections every so often to relieve the suffering.

The removed tissue went to two different labs to be checked for signs of cancer. Four days later I left the hospital feeling fine and praising God for His great goodness toward me. Another three days went by, and I went to Dr. Wise's office to find out the results of the tests. When I entered, he was all smiles and excited. "No traces of cancer have been found," he reported, then explained how fortunate I was in light of the earlier tests.

Thanking him, I reminded him that after the first tests I had requested to know exactly how critical my situation was. I had wanted to know my condition, I explained, so I would know how I needed to pray. "Now I thank you for being honest with me, and most of all I thank God for doing what was humanly impossible."

Shocking News

About six months later I received a call from California. It was Cyril Grosse, the man who had led me from spirit worship to Christ. After we had chatted a few minutes, he mentioned that he had some bad news to tell me.

"This may shock you," he said, "but according to my doctor I have only about six months to live. The biopsies have revealed that I have advanced prostate cancer. It has spread to adjoining organs, including the lymph nodes. The doctor says that he will have to do drastic surgery as well as radiation treatments. It may even involve castration."

While the news was bad, it did not throw me into a state of despondency. After all, I had passed through a similar situation only a few months before. God had brought me through it, and I believed that He would do the same for my close friend.

I suggested that he try to postpone the surgery for about three weeks and use the time to enlist the prayers of people he knew to be men and women of strong faith. Of course I added that Hilda and I would also pray for him.

Cyril liked my suggestion, and the doctor went along with his request for a short delay in the surgery. At the end of the three weeks the specialist ran tests that showed a definite improvement in my friend's condition. He told Cyril to return in another three weeks. To the doctor's surprise, the next set of tests showed that a number of the smaller tumors had vanished, and the cancer was in remission.

Every three months Cyril went to the specialist. In October the doctor suggested that the enlarged prostate should be removed in order to restore normal urinary function. The operation was a success, and laboratory analysis revealed only a tiny trace of the cancer remaining in the center of the organ.

Subsequent examinations have shown Cyril to be free of cancer, and my friend is back teaching in his classroom.

A Call for Help

One of my brothers, Edmond, lived in Ottawa. Shortly after my first book on intercessory prayer came off the press, he bought more than 50 copies and sent them to relatives and friends. One copy went to his ex-wife, who lived in Niagara Falls, Ontario.

Impressed by the stories of how God had responded to prayer, she phoned Edmond and asked if he would be willing to contact me and request that I pray about a bone disease that was progressively crippling her.

She had suffered from the painful condition for a number of years. At first a bone deformity had appeared between her ankle and heel, creating a lump that had enlarged to the point that she could no longer wear a shoe. It had also become so painful that she couldn't put any weight on her foot, and had to use crutches.

When the pain became so severe that even powerful medications could no longer block it, the doctors began seriously thinking of amputating her foot. But shortly after I began praying for her, the pain diminished and in a few days vanished completely. The lump began to shrink, and before long she could wear a shoe again.

Since then she has been able to shop and do other activities that people had once been doing for her. She has especially appreciated being able to visit some of her children living in northern Ontario.

10
NO GREATER JOY

Since the publication of my first book on intercessory prayer, hundreds of individuals have written or telephoned to tell how the Spirit of God has blessed their lives as they read about the power of intercessory prayer and began to put it into practice.

My prayer list has constantly increased as I have joined my prayers to their intercessions before God. The Lord has greatly honored us as the Holy Spirit has given people victory over self, over sin, over temptation, and over the power of fallen angels.

And the one thing that most surprises those praying people is how the Spirit of God gets individuals who have no use for God or spiritual things to suddenly have a change of heart. God has used their prayers to work miracles. They then write me long letters telling of the joy they are experiencing.

For example, let me share a few excerpts from letters by a woman I will call Mary Brown.

"Dear Brother Morneau:

"What a joy to serve our Lord in prayer ministry. During the past two years I have come to believe very strongly in intercessory prayer. Also during that same period I have been seeking a closer walk with Jesus and ways to serve Him more fully each day. He has led and guided me so wonderfully, and your book was a part of that special guidance.

"I have adopted some of your 'proven' ideas. I especially like the one of asking for God to surround my prayer subject with an atmosphere of light and peace. Let me briefly share one prayer experience.

"My sister Josephine, 38 years of age, had an affair, and her husband left as a result. She went through 'hell' (her word) for more than two months after Russell moved out. Although she did not realize it, he had known about the affair for more than a year. She had been pressuring her lover to choose between her or his own wife.

"Up to that time she had never in any way indicated that she felt any need of God or religion. But when this crisis came, she turned to me and asked that I pray for her. I prayed fervently that her lover would stay with his wife. Two months later he emphatically told her that he would never leave his wife, and then ended the affair.

"Some time later I learned that both Josephine and Russell were both praying that they would soon be back together again.

"What a thrill to be used of our dear heavenly Father in such a special work. It is my desire and prayer to become a wise intercessor and to be used more and more by my Master in this precious responsibility. To see how God answers prayer is so exciting. My faith grows steadily. I have adopted the prayer idea you mention on page 48 of your book. What a wonderful, blessing-filled idea.

"The Lord has been good to me. I have several very dear friends, and instead of giving you a few names to place on your prayer list every time I write, I decided to send them all at once. I shall let you know as providence unfolds in each of their lives.

"I have adopted for my personal petition each morning the beautiful prayer you shared on page 27. . . .

"Today I am mailing a copy of your book to my parents. The Lord has given me wonderful witnessing opportunities with them. They have just recently started going to church, and as Mom put it, they will 'try' different ones to see which they like best. They are truly searching, and as they do, I pray every day. I really believe with all my heart that our Lord will 'bring them in.' It is just a matter of time. That will be a most glorious occasion that I anticipate with great joy.

"I promise to pray for you and yours each day until our dear Jesus comes to take us home. What a blessed, awesome day that will be.

"Have a pleasant, happy day."

Three months later I received another letter from her.

"Dear Brother and Sister Morneau:

"Thank you, Hilda, for your precious note. I have some wonderful prayer answers to share again. If you will recall, I asked you last time to please pray for my sister, whose marriage had broken up. They are back together. Her husband came home the week of Christmas, and they are both working to make a go of it. Praise God!

"Another answer to prayer has been the miracle I have seen in my stepdad's life. Even three months ago I would have never dreamed that I would be sitting beside my parents in church. What a thrill that was. I see before my eyes the working of the Holy Spirit in their lives, and that gives me great courage."

Each day I grow more excited over the fact that great numbers of Christians are pleading for God to extend the merits of Christ's sacrifice to those in need. One person wrote to me, "I became deeply impressed with the importance and great value you are placing on the shed blood of Christ being appropriated to those we pray for. I now take time every day to talk with our heavenly Father about my appreciation of the power to save found in the merits of the divine blood of Christ, and for the Holy Spirit to work out a great salvation in their lives. I am seeing my prayers being answered before my eyes, and that is most wonderful!"

I believe that we are beginning to witness the fulfillment of the words of Isaiah about the closing of God's work in the earth: "Arise, shine; for thy light is come, and the glory of the Lord is risen upon thee. For, behold, the darkness shall cover the earth, and gross darkness the people: but the Lord shall arise upon thee, and his glory shall be seen upon thee. And the Gentiles shall come to thy light, and kings to the brightness of thy rising" (Isaiah 60:1-3).

As I read letters from people who are having their intercessory prayers answered, I notice that they also grasp with new clarity that only the Holy Spirit can make and keep the human heart pure.

Long ago I prayed that I would find my greatest joy in asking the Spirit of God to bless the lives of those whose names were on my perpetual prayer list. Before long I saw the Holy Spirit at work in my life as I frequently thought of those who needed the blessing of God in their lives.

I discovered the joy of praying as I drove my car, as I walked to business calls, as I waited for people who had made appointments with me. And the results delighted me. For example, I would pray for those of my business clients whom I knew were struggling with problems. When I would later visit them, they would spontaneously tell me how God had blessed them.

God's blessing of others continues to this day. Permit me to tell of an experience that had happened just as I was writing this chapter.

Mary's Story

A young woman whom I will name Mary had phoned to request that I pray for a friend who had just moments before left her husband for another man. In tears she had told how the friend, whom I will call Betty, had once prayed for her when Mary had had marital problems. In fact, Betty had even contacted me and requested that I pray for Mary. Now it was Mary's turn to seek someone to intercede with God for Betty's salvation.

Although I instantly recognized the name, I let Mary do the talking. Without my prompting her in any way Mary told about the struggles she had gone through. "Jim and I were married a little more than two years and still very much in love," she said. "He was doing graduate study and our income was quite limited, so we were happy when I got a better-paying job that seemed the answer to prayer."

She paused a moment, then asked, "Mr. Morneau, do you think that it is possible for a woman to fall in love with another man even when she is still deeply in love with her husband?"

Instead of slipping into a discussion of genuine love and the power of infatuation, I simply replied that in this day and age many strange things have taken place. "I don't know why I am telling you this," Mary continued, "except that I believe the Holy Spirit wants you to see how the Holy Spirit answered your prayers for me.

"After I had been at my new job in a large department store for a couple months, I began to notice one of the managers. His kindness and habit of complimenting me caught my attention. I began to like him very much.

"Before long I could not get him out of my mind. I found myself thinking about him constantly, even when

I was with my husband. Although I realized that it was wrong for me to let him continually occupy my thoughts, I simply couldn't stop it. His power over me was so great that one day I found myself admitting to Betty that if the man asked me to go to bed with him, I would not be able to resist.

"I knew that was exactly what would happen if things kept on going the way they were. Just a few days before, I had discovered myself hoping that he would put his arms around me while we were alone together in a warehouse area.

"At times he had placed a hand on my arm as we talked, and a powerful and most enjoyable sensation had coursed through my entire body. I was getting totally hooked on him. But, thank God, you, Mr. Morneau, and Betty were praying for me. When the day came that he invited me to his apartment to see the stamp collection that was his pride and joy, I automatically replied, 'Oh, I couldn't do that without my husband being with me.'

"Then a tide of fear flooded through my mind as I realized what would take place in his apartment if I were alone with him. A passage I had memorized as a child—Joseph's words when he was faced with temptation—flashed through my mind: 'How then can I do this great wickedness, and sin against God?' Suddenly I was now afraid of something that until that moment I had been longing for.

"I am not exaggerating, Mr. Morneau, when I say that in those few moments I regained my sense of right and wrong. The shackles of infatuation fell off me, and by the grace of God I will never wear them again."

I reminded Mary that people had been making intercessions with God on her behalf. The Holy Spirit had been moving mightily in her time of need. She did not say anything for 10 or 15 seconds, but I could hear her sobbing. Finally, regaining her composure, she thanked me for my prayers for her.

But the reason for her call was still troubling her. She could not understand why the woman who had prayed for her during Mary's time of need should now herself suddenly move in with another man. "How can a person like Betty, one that I always considered to be a strong Christian, fall into sin so totally that she will not listen to reason? Her outlook on life has changed so greatly that spiritual things don't seem to matter to her anymore.

"It scares me when I think of it, and I keep asking myself, 'if Betty, always before a person of strong principles, can suddenly give up on spiritual things, what chance do I have of making it to heaven?'"

"You are not the only person who has asked me that kind of question," I replied. "In fact, a great number of people have written to me with prayer requests for someone's marriage. People constantly tell me of their shock when they see someone they have considered a pillar of the church suddenly throw his or her marriage away."

A tone of urgency filled her voice as she asked me what I thought was happening to the church. I explained that I believed that such people had not learned how to be "kept by the power of God through faith" (1 Peter 1:5), and that widespread adultery and marital breakup was the consequence of church members slowly releasing their hold upon God until the natural inclinations of the fallen human heart overwhelmed them.

"Turning away from something as sacred as wedding vows," I told her, "makes no sense unless we remember that the fallen human 'heart is deceitful above all things, and desperately wicked' [Jeremiah 17:9]. In fact, it is so deceptive that even Solomon, the wisest of all human beings and thrice called by Scripture beloved of God, ruined his life when he forgot to keep God always before him. He soon discovered the power of unbridled infatuation. The Bible says that 'his wives turned away his heart after other gods. . . . Then did

Solomon build an high place for Chemosh, the abomination of Moab, in the hill that is before Jerusalem, and for Molech. . . . And likewise did he for all his strange wives, which burnt incense and sacrificed unto their gods' [1 Kings 11:4-8]."

Mary wanted to know more about being "kept by the power of God through faith." I promised to write a letter in which I would explain about the power of sin and separation from God, and how helpless we are against such forces unless the Spirit of God intervenes.

In the chapters to follow I will present some of the important factors that we need to know to preserve our vital relationship with God. Also, I will show how our prayers for another can allow God to send the Holy Spirit more fully to fight our loved ones' battles against sin and evil.

UNLIMITED HELP

Living victorious and successful Christian lives is the all-important thing, and we can do it only one way—through the Spirit of God resting upon us and dwelling in us.

The apostle Paul, writing to the Ephesians for whose salvation he had labored so diligently, caught their attention by stressing the kind of prayer he did for them. "For this cause I bow my knees unto the Father of our Lord Jesus Christ . . . that he would grant you, according to the riches of his glory, to be strengthened with might by his Spirit in the inner man; that Christ may dwell in your hearts by faith; that ye, being rooted and grounded in love, may be able to comprehend with all saints what is the breadth, and length, and depth, and height; and to know the love of Christ, which passeth knowledge, that ye might be filled with all the fulness of God" (Ephesians 3:14-19).

Those few lines must have been a wonderful encouragement to the Christians at Ephesus as they realized that Paul had been praying for the Holy Spirit to strengthen them in a special way. Only then could they live victorious Christian lives in this fallen world.

To understand the impact that Paul's prayer had on them we must remember that the Ephesians had at one time been anything but model individuals. Ephesians 2:1, 2 declared of them, "And you hath he quickened, who were dead in trespasses and sins; wherein in time past ye walked according to the course of this world, according to the prince of the power of the air, the spirit that now worketh in the children of disobedience."

A number of the Ephesians had even been deeply involved in the supernatural. Acts 19:19 tells us, "Many of them also which used curious arts brought their books together, and burned them before all men: and they counted the price of them, and found it fifty thousand pieces of silver."

Convicted by the Holy Spirit, these practitioners of the occult burned manuscripts worth a fortune and yielded their lives to Christ. I can imagine that Paul and his 12 companions (mentioned at the beginning of the chapter) must have done some serious praying for these men and women.

I believe that they prayed both for God to appropriate the merits of the blood Christ shed at Calvary, and for the Spirit of God to surround each one with a divine atmosphere of peace and spiritual light. And it could well be that they asked God to have the Holy Spirit overpower and nullify the power of sin, the power of death, and the power of separation from God in each believer's life. Surely Paul and his friends must have made this kind of prayer daily.

Fantastic conversions took place among the Ephesians, and I am persuaded by the Word of God that similar and far more numerous conversions will happen when God's people intercede with God for others with a faith as determined as that Paul and his friends had.

In 1946, after the Holy Spirit converted me from spiritualism to Christianity, the Epistle to the Ephesians became a great source of encouragement to me—especially when I realized what Paul's prayer had accomplished among those who had been involved in the occult. Ephesians 2:4-7 has never failed to amaze me. "But God, who is rich in mercy, for his great love wherewith he loved us, even when we were dead in sins, hath quickened us together with Christ, (by grace ye are saved;) . . . that in the ages to come he might shew the exceeding riches of his grace, in his kindness toward us, through Christ Jesus." We will be the demonstration and showcase before the rest of the universe of His forgiveness and ability to transform rebellious sinners.

The Spirit of God strengthened the early Christians, enabling them to become something they otherwise could not. It alone empowered them to live successful Christian lives. And according to the apostle John, heaven blessed their prayer life, the secret of their victorious Christianity. "Whatsoever we ask, we receive of him, because we keep his commandments, and do those things that are pleasing in his sight" (1 John 3:22). They were able to keep His commandments because their prayer life opened up to them the power of the Holy Spirit, as we witness over and over in the New Testament.

Acts 3 records how Peter and John visited the Temple in Jerusalem at the daily hour of prayer. As they approached one of the gates, a lame beggar stopped them and asked them for money. "Then Peter said, Silver and gold have I none; but such as I have give I thee: In the name of Jesus Christ of Nazareth rise up and walk" (verse 6). The Bible states that the crippled man's feet and ankles received healing and strength, and he began to leap and praise God.

It is my firm conviction that God will again demonstrate such miracles among His people, but right now we are still in the process of acquiring genuine biblical faith. Such faith is a must before He can honor our prayers as He did the disciples and other early Christians. Such biblical faith consists of three elements:

1. Belief in God.
2. Trust in God.
3. Loyalty to God.

Jesus—Lord of the Impossible

Shortly after the publication of my first book on intercessory prayer, a woman wrote, "I have a son that needs the kind of praying that you talked about in your book. I would like very much to talk to you about him, if you would be kind enough to send me your phone number. It would be so much easier to tell you about his problem over the phone. Please help me! A sister in Christ."

A few days later I received a phone call from her. She explained that she and her husband had a 32-year-old son named Henry who by the age of 20 had apparently lost almost all his mental faculties because of drug use. Since then he had been unable to take care of himself. He would sit in a chair for as long as three hours at a time, silently smoking and staring at a wall. Sometimes Henry's eyes would follow his mother as she cooked or moved around the kitchen. The son had no sense of day or night, and when he did sleep, it was only for short periods of time. Occasionally he would slap himself with great force in the face or on his arms or legs until he turned black and blue.

When told not to hurt himself, Henry would explode into rage and insist that no one should speak to him. He had let his hair grow down to the middle of his back, refusing to allow anyone to cut it. The man seemed unable to recognize even his parents, and his speech was unintelligible. At times he would talk to himself in a series of grunts. His parents considered his condition hopeless.

After I had listened to Mrs. Harvey (not her real name) for about 20 minutes, I began to wonder why she was asking me for help in a situation that appeared even beyond the aid of medical science. Then I realized that it wasn't me that mattered here, but God. The woman was trying to reach out to God through me. Perhaps the Lord could use me to lead her to the Holy Spirit and His life-giving power. Perhaps the Holy Spirit was waiting to re-create the son's mental faculties, thereby exalting Christ and strengthening the faith of many.

Silently I asked God to bless my mind with what I should say to her. After conversing with her awhile, I assured her that I would take Henry's case to heart. I would place his name on my prayer list and pray for him in a special way. Also I requested that she periodically keep me posted on his condition.

Time went by, and one day I received a letter from her telling me that Henry was beginning to improve. His speech had become clearer, and—to his parents' surprise—he had asked his mother to cut his hair for the first time in 16 years. Mrs. Harvey was elated, and she stated that her and her husband's faith was growing stronger as they saw the Spirit of God blessing their son's life.

Offering my own thanksgiving to God, I pointed her to biblical incidents in which the Lord had done wonderful things for His people.

A few months later Henry decided to stop smoking. When he announced his intention, his mother figured that because he had been a chain smoker for so many years, he would be unable to quit. She had known too many people who had tried and failed.

But to his parents' astonishment, Henry never touched a cigarette again. Mrs. Harvey waited a month before writing me about it. For the next six or seven months she sent me a monthly report, and to my joy she and her husband gave God all the credit for all the changes in their son's life. Yet one thing still bothered her—God wasn't restoring his mind as they had hoped for. One additional letter arrived. In it Mrs. Harvey admitted that her faith in God's power to help them was beginning to waver. Naturally I prayed that her faith would not fail her. When we seek a special blessing from God, the Bible says, "Let him ask in faith, nothing wavering. For he that wavereth is like a wave of the sea driven with the wind and tossed. For let not that man think that he shall receive any thing of the Lord" (James 1:6, 7).

About 11:00 in the evening not more than 10 days later Mrs. Harvey called me. She could barely talk because of crying. With a quick silent prayer for help, I managed to calm her down to the point where I could make out what she was saying. It seemed that Henry had unexpectedly become violent, throwing chairs through the windows and threatening to beat up his father. They had had to call the sheriff's department and have the son taken to a mental institution. She informed me that she had lost all hope of her son ever getting better. "I am sorry to tell you this," she said, "but I have lost faith in the power of prayer, and will no longer trouble God with my needs."

Telling her not to give up, I said that I would redouble my intercessions for her son. I believed that his violent reaction had been brought on by the forces of darkness. They were trying to get us to quit praying for Henry. Before she hung up I left her with a few verses of Scripture to think about.

It wasn't many days later that she called again. This time her voice vibrated with happiness as she praised God for a mighty miracle of divine grace. Henry was back home healthy both in mind and body. Although he could remember nothing that had taken place during the past 12 years, he was out visiting old friends, neighbors, and relatives with his father.

When I asked Mrs. Harvey how it had happened, she said her son had awakened one morning at the mental institution feeling perfectly well. The doctors found him mentally alert, and after a day or two phoned his parents to come get their wonderfully transformed son.

"Glory to God in the highest!" I shouted over the phone, and rejoiced with her over how God still shows His love for us.

12
THE TRAGEDY OF CRUMBLING HOMES

A spiritual plague has been devastating the lives of men, women, and children around the world. It afflicts both young and old, but especially brings misery to innocent children who can't begin to understand why Mother and Dad can no longer get along, and one of them is now moving out.

The past couple decades have seen a climate that desensitizes the mind to one's responsibilities as a spouse and parent. Satan and his angels are working with all the various forces of today's society to destroy the natural affection that the Creator planted in each human being. They permeate our culture with sexual imagery and expose everyone to all kinds of immorality. In this day and age, unless a person makes constant and determined daily requests for God's help to remain pure in thought, heart, and life, even the most self-disciplined individual may imperceptibly become corrupt at heart, and suddenly fall like a rotten oak tree. Permit me to illustrate.

"My husband and I are in our 50s," a woman wrote to me one day, "have raised a family, worked hard to educate our children, and brought them up in the admonition of the Lord. Our grown children have married well, have established homes that are under the blessing of God. I have always been committed to church activities, and enjoyed serving the Lord.

"My husband was first elder of our large church, and lived what we all thought was an exemplary life. He was looked upon as a pillar in the church until about six months ago when it was discovered that he had been secretly enjoying a girlie magazine and pornographic videotapes.

"His evil interest was revealed in the following way. Friends of ours who live in a rural area had been having difficulties with their 20-year-old daughter who was attending a community college. They had discussed the problem with us, and we agreed that Reta (not her name) could live with us, where she could then attend a Christian college.

"All went well until one evening I attended a meeting that ended about an hour earlier than usual. Arriving home, I unexpectedly found my husband in bed with Reta. Since then the whole thing has been like a nightmare.

"My husband has moved to another area, is still shacking up with that innocent-looking girl, and has just informed me that he wants a divorce. He is a changed man, but not for the better. Now he doesn't care about me, about the church, not even about the fact that he has hurt the lives of a great many persons. It is too bad that such a thing took place in our lives. We had reached the point where there were no longer any college tuition bills to meet, no real problems to worry about. My husband and I had been able to set aside quite a lot of money for our retirement, and were looking forward to enjoying the golden years of our lives.

"The thing that makes it so difficult to adjust to my great loss is that my husband had been a man of principle all through his life. I considered him to be as solid as the Rock of Gibraltar when it came to standing firmly for right. It is sad to say, but I was wrong.

"Our two married sons have stopped going to church, and that has brought great distress to the lives of their wives and children."

The woman, after giving me additional information on the problem, requested that I pray for each member of her family. She is hurting and wonders if she could have done anything prayerwise to avert such a tragedy.

In another case a wife wrote how her 60-year-old husband had gotten sexually involved with their 17-year-old foster daughter. Again the husband moved out and is living together with the girl. Head deacon in his church, he greatly shocked many people by his actions. His wife wondered if he could suddenly have become mentally unbalanced. She asked that I pray for all three involved, because she still wants her husband to be in Christ's kingdom. And she too, like so many others who have had such tragedies strike them, wondered if there was a particular way she could have prayed to prevent such a thing happening in her husband's life.

Before I explain what I term *preventative praying*, I would like to say that over the years I have been an attentive student of human nature. I have always been interested in knowing what compels a person to do something that he or she later deeply regrets. For 20 years I was in telephone directory (yellow pages) advertising sales. Year after year I would call back on the same businesspeople, and they learned to trust me and often began to confide their problems to me.

From what they told me about their lives, I discovered that though a man may have been brought up to practice self-control and to be temperate in all things, when the media, Satan, or anything else begins to influence his imagination toward an attractive female, it will not take long before he is willing to risk all, to throw everything away, to indulge in his fantasies.

A spiritist priest once claimed to me that demon spirits can flash thought images into people's minds to influence them in a particular direction. How Satan could do this we do not know, but we all recognize how evil influences—whatever their source—sway people. If men (and women) start dwelling upon such evil suggestions, they soon start creating a bright and exciting picture in their minds of what it would be like if only they put that idea into practice.

The more a person plays with the idea or suggestion, the more powerful and realistic it becomes. Soon it can take control of the mind to the point where an individual will find himself or herself doing things he or she knows shouldn't be done. Demon spirits or other influences can take control of the life until nothing on the human level can break the hold.

Because of the deceptive power of sin a Christian spouse should be willing to do some serious *preventative praying* regardless of how faithful the husband or wife has been to his or her marriage vows. No matter how noble a Christian one has been, it is still possible to fall. Even Satan was a sinless being.

Every day it is good to thank God for having blessed a loved one with grace and strength, for having imparted to him or her divine compassionate love. Only when a person possesses the love of Christ can he or she display toward a fellow human being the heavenly graces that adorn the character of our great Redeemer.

The spouse who wants to spend eternity with his or her husband, as well as have him or her in the present life, must secure the stabilizing influence of the Holy Spirit, that great divine power that alone can impart purity of thought, heart, and life. While God never forces anyone to do anything against his or her will, He will, because of the merits of the blood Christ shed on the cross, do everything possible to protect and lead a person toward salvation. Christ tells us always to "pray one for another."

Over the past few years many letters have arrived from husbands and wives in shaky marriages. After I have shared with them these principles, the Spirit of God administered to their spouses the graces of redemption and solidified their union in Christ. Nothing can be more rewarding than to hear again from those same individuals how the Lord has blessed in joyous and surprising ways.

Lost and Found

Here is an outstanding illustration of how the stabilizing influence of the Holy Spirit can restore spiritually wayward individuals.

Shortly after my first prayer book came off the press, I received a letter from a woman whose husband had left her almost four years before. She was particularly impressed by the fact that before I pray for a person who does not serve God, I first ask that the Father will appropriate the merits of Christ's blood to the person in need, always conscious that the individual's redemption has already been paid for.

"When I read in your book that we can pray for the Lord to forgive another's sins," she said, "I was astounded, and began praying for my husband with new faith and hope."

She said that she and her husband were both in their 30s, had good jobs and health, and had looked forward to a bright future. Employed by a multinational corporation, the man spoke three languages, which quickly propelled him up the corporate ladder.

"Before long the demands of the job began to take him away from home days at a time. It wasn't long before the lavish lifestyle of the corporate world began making its mark on him. Even his character was changing in that he became quite critical of me, and seemed to be looking for occasions to disagree on most everything I said.

"He began to criticize the church and its people, and the time came that I found myself going to church alone. As time passed he began wearing expensive jewelry, and not long after I became aware that he was smoking. And when he was brought home drunk from a Christmas party, he added to my disappointment by stating that he was also having an affair with his secretary.

"Our home became a place of contention and unrest. At that time I thanked the Lord that we didn't have any children to be torn apart by the terrible discord. I did all I could to have us seek the help of a Christian counselor, but to no avail. In fact, he moved out and blamed me for breaking up our home."

In a telephone conversation she told me that she didn't hear about him for almost two years. Then she found out that he was in deep trouble with his employer. He had made several decisions that had caused the corporation to lose vast amounts of money. Before long the company terminated him, and he left the area so that she lost track of him. His experience at the multinational corporation now made it impossible to obtain similar employment, which drove him to heavy drinking.

Later she found out that he tried gambling and was successful at it for a time. Next he got involved in drugs, causing him to lose control of his life and everything he possessed. He thought of killing himself, "but discovered that he didn't have what it took to carry on with his plan. That was most shocking to his manhood to realize that he was some kind of coward," his wife told me.

Meanwhile she acquired a copy of my book, read it, and was especially impressed with the chapter "Praying for the Ungodly and the Wicked." She wrote to ask if I would join her in praying for her husband, whom she hoped was still alive.

I wrote back to assure her that the Holy Spirit would surely minister the graces of redemption to the man as she and I sought God's help.

Knowing what both the demons and Christ were determined to do in this man's life, I became bolder in my determination that Satan would not have his way, but that Christ would. With this man, as with everyone else I pray for, I relied on the mighty power of the Holy Spirit to overpower, and render nonoperative, the enemies of Jesus Christ and all those He is determined to save.

I assured the woman that I would put both her and her husband's name on my perpetual prayer list. Daily and without fail I would present them before Jesus. I asked only that she keep me posted on what was happening in their lives.

About a year went by. Then one evening she had on the national television news as it interviewed a group of homeless people in a distant city. The people were living in the back of an abandoned factory under a highway overpass. The state wanted to demolish their shacks and move them elsewhere.

As she was cooking, she heard a familiar voice. Turning around, she saw her husband on the screen. If he had not spoken, she would have never recognized him. He wore a beard and had long hair down his back and, she said, "looked like a tramp. He was a pitiful sight."

When he stated that he obtained most of his food from the garbage cans behind restaurants, she burst into tears. It broke her heart. Despite her deep sorrow, she was thankful that he was still alive, and that fact gave her hope of better things to come.

The next day she contacted the news network and learned where the interview had been done. Arranging to have some time off from work, she began her search for her husband.

But some time later as she steered her car between shacks and old broken-down machinery to reach a group of men warming themselves by a fire in a steel barrel, she began to worry about her safety and made sure that her car was carefully locked.

One of the men told her what shack to go to, adding that it had no door. She would have to wedge her way between a large piece of heavy canvas and the shack to reach the opening.

The woman found her husband in his 8 x 10-foot shack, lying on a pile of broken-down cardboard boxes about 20 inches in height that he used to insulate himself from the cold of the pavement. As he got up to let some more light into the place, she threw herself into his arms, saying, "I will never let you go!"

Stunned by her action, he kept repeating, "Please let me go. I am filthy—I am disgustingly filthy."

It was late autumn in that distant eastern city, and a light snow was failing. Getting cold, she invited him to sit with her in her car. Refusing to enter the car lest he dirty it, he stood by the door while she kept the window partly down. As the snow continued to fall, he soon resembled a snowman.

Would he sit in the car if she covered the seat with a blanket? she asked. When he said he would, she drove off, to return 45 minutes later with a car blanket and an abundance of hot food from a fast-food restaurant. The sight of him feasting on what he considered food fit for a king brought joy to her heart. Silently she sent a melody of praise ascending to God for bringing her husband back into her life. She believed that God was marvelously answering her prayers.

It took a whole week of talking before he agreed to resume living with her. She discovered that once a person's life has deteriorated to the degree his had, only special divine grace can transform it back again.

When at the end of the first day she had not succeeded in getting him out of his shack, she returned to her motel. That evening she did much praying, and sought special guidance on how to handle the situation. She desperately wanted him to resume a normal life again. Before retiring for the night, she opened her Bible for something to meditate upon. Glancing down at the right-hand page, her eyes fell upon the following words:

"If the Spirit of him that raised up Jesus from the dead dwell in you, he that raised up Christ from the dead shall also quicken your mortal bodies by his Spirit that dwelleth in you" (Romans 8:11).

"That's it," she said to herself. "My husband's mind needs to be re-created by the power of the Spirit of God to what it once was—to the degree of sanity that he once possessed." Down on her knees she went, pouring out her heart to God.

Five days passed, and everything seemed at a standstill.

Then an idea entered her mind. *What my husband needs is to hear of God's power and love operating in people's behalf in these modern times. I will read him portions of Morneau's book.*

That she did, and God began to work through those feeble words. Slowly he began to respond to the Spirit and her suggestions that she and he could still have a bright future together if they would make God first in their lives.

"I couldn't stop the tears from running down my face as I listened to him talk, and realized that the Holy Spirit was bringing my husband back from the dead. He had died spiritually, and now he was alive again, telling me of the joy that he once had when serving God."

Then she received the shock of her life when he said, "OK, Linda (not her real name), I accept your invitation for us to live once again as husband and wife. That is, if you can get transferred by your company to a city where no one knows us. I couldn't face people who knew me in the past. Meanwhile you will have me stay a few miles out of town—am I right?"

Again she assured him that she would do all that she had promised earlier. It took another couple of days to persuade him to go to a barber shop, to clothing stores, and to clean himself up so that he could live like a normal person once more.

So it was by the mighty outworkings of the Holy Spirit that Linda obtained a transfer to another city, and to her great surprise, it was a promotion that involved a substantial increase in pay. Both are now living happily together in the Lord. Both their Christian walks have, she says, matured under the nurturing of the Spirit of God.

Private people, Linda had once asked me that I never tell anyone about her husband's experience. I had promised to abide by her wishes. However, more recently I began to feel that I should ask permission to include it in this book as a means of exalting our Saviour's love and power. They agreed as long as I did not mention their names or where the events had taken place. I believe their experience gives glory to God in the highest!

A PRAYER MINISTRY

Perhaps the question people most ask me is "How can a person begin a successful prayer ministry and keep it going? One that will enable me to actually see my prayers answered?"

I have discovered five steps to follow that have demonstrated that they will bring the power of God into the lives of those you pray for.

Step 1: The key to any successful prayer ministry begins with having a closer walk with Jesus. He is the chief soul winner, and longs to help each one of us to share in His mission. For me that walk with Jesus begins as soon as I open my eyes in the morning, even before I get out of bed. My morning prayer goes something like this:

"Precious Jesus, Thou Lord of glory, I am looking up to the Holy of Holies of the heavenly sanctuary where You are ministering in behalf of fallen humanity, and I seek from Your hand at the beginning of this day a fresh unction of Your love and grace.

"As You are well aware, Lord, my fallen nature is such that if left to myself I will only produce all kinds of wicked deeds that would lead to my eternal destruction. Therefore, I cry unto Thee, Lord, please appropriate to me at this moment the merits of the blood that You shed at Calvary for the remission of sins.

"I wish for You to mold me, to fashion me, to raise me into a pure and holy atmosphere where the rich currents of Your love may flow through my soul, and in turn bless those I encounter in this land of Your enemy.

"I pray, precious Redeemer, for Thy Holy Spirit to rest upon me, and to dwell in me this day, and to make me like Thyself in character. Thank You for being attentive to my prayers. Amen."

After getting up and attending to my early morning needs—such as letting the dog out, etc.—I then have my devotions. They usually consist of reading the Bible and some other inspiring material that will lead me to additional conversation in prayer with Jesus. Only then do I present before Him my prayer list (which by now has filled up hundreds of pages in record books).

Each name in the list has an accompanying description of his or her needs. While it is impossible to mention every person individually, each day I do present a great number by name as the Spirit of God brings them to my attention. But I pray for the great spiritual needs of all my people in the way that I believe that the apostle Paul prayed for the church members at Ephesus.

After breakfast I converse in prayer with my heavenly Father, praising His name, and giving thanks for the infinite mercies He has showered upon the lives of those I have been praying for. I appreciate and thank God for the fact that I am retired and thus have so much time to carry on my prayer ministry.

Step 2: A solid foundation is a must if one expects to erect any edifice that will be able to stand the test of time. The same principle applies to the spiritual realm.

To build an unfaltering trust in God and in the power of His Holy Spirit, we must memorize the Word of God. We must fill our minds with scriptures that will encourage, inspire, uplift, and, above all, draw one's heart to Him. As we do this, we open the way for the Holy Spirit later to bring them to mind in times of need. The Word of God is a divine avenue of power and life.

I am speaking here from experience. Over the past 46 years I have carried in my coat pocket pieces of paper upon which I have copied verses of Scripture to memorize during my leisure time. During that time I have committed more than 2,200 verses to memory, immeasurably enriching my spiritual life. I invite you to steep yourself in Scripture. If you do, you will produce prayers that will pay high dividends in souls.

Step 3: Compassionate love motivated Christ to come to this rebellious planet and let wicked men nail Him to a cross—all so He could obtain eternal life for each one of us.

Christ had a love for His children that was boundless. Jesus was a caring person in the fullest sense of the term. He wants you and me to share that same compulsion. We need to pray with the greatest possible intensity and desire that He will endow us with that same motivating force.

Step 4: To pray for others, we must absolutely have a living faith. Christ's question. "When the Son of man cometh, shall he find faith on the earth?" (Luke 18:8) suggests that it may be a rare experience during the last days, but successful prayer for others is impossible without it.

As we read the four Gospels, we soon notice that the measure of the miracles that Christ could do for others was in relation to the amount of faith they exercised. For instance, the Bible tells us that two blind men followed Jesus, begging for mercy upon themselves. Matthew 9:29, 30 declares, "Then touched he their eyes, saying, According to your faith be it unto you. And their eyes were opened."

Matthew 4:23, 24 tells us that "Jesus went about all Galilee, . . . healing all manner of sickness and all manner of disease among the people. And his fame went throughout all Syria: and they brought unto him all sick people that were taken with divers diseases and torments, and those which were possessed with devils, and those which were lunatick, and those that had the palsy; and he healed them."

On the other hand, people with a low level of faith actually robbed themselves of blessings. Matthew 13:58 reminds us that "he did not many mighty works there because of their unbelief." So it is with our prayers for others—we must seek and maintain a high level of faith.

Step 5: Forgiveness makes the difference.

We live in an age where people do not find their prayers answered because they have not first asked God to forgive their own sins. It is my firm practice never to pray for a person unless I raise my heart to God in this way: "Dear heavenly Father, in the name of the Lord Jesus, please forgive me if I have offended Thee in thought, word, or deed. I know, Lord, that Your hand is not shortened that it cannot save, neither Your ear heavy that it cannot hear, but I realize that our iniquities and sins can separate us from Thee and Thy rich blessings [see Isaiah 59:1, 2]. I can't afford to be separated from Thee even for a moment, so please make everything right between Thee and me, I pray."

A large number of Christians mentioned in their letters and phone calls that their prayers seemed to be going nowhere. They asked me what I thought the problem was. First I tried to help by questioning them about their Christian life. But that approach seemed to be a dead end. Finally I asked the Lord to have the Holy Spirit help me to understand the problem.

Before I went to bed that particular night I opened

the Bible for something to meditate on before I fell asleep. When I flipped it open I saw the Lord's Prayer. I did not stop there, however, but continued reading. "If ye forgive men their trespasses, your heavenly Father will also forgive you: but if ye forgive not men their trespasses, neither will your Father forgive your trespasses" (Matthew 6:14, 15).

Instantly it occurred to me that the unforgiving attitude of some people could be blocking the way of God's blessings. Since then I have helped many individuals by asking if they have any difficulty in forgiving the shortcomings of others or the wrongs those individuals may have done them.

One woman was puzzled why her prayers seemed so ineffectual. When I brought up this possible attitude, she instantly stated that that was her problem. "In fact," she said, "it's a characteristic that runs in our family. I will always remember my granddad saying, 'if anybody does anything hurtful to you, don't get mad—just wait for the right opportunity, and get even with that person.'" She then admitted that only a miracle of God in her life would enable her to forgive others.

About six months later she called again. But this time rejoicing filled her voice as she told how God had given her the capacity to truly forgive others. And now her prayers were producing beautiful results.

FEELING UNFORGIVEN

The hundreds of letters that God-loving people have sent since February 1990 reveal a most distressing pattern. They indicate that a great number of people evaluate their relationship with God almost totally by their feelings.

At times some of them feel God is far away from them. Others conclude that their prayers don't really amount to much, so they will go all day without praying. And many others can't figure out what's keeping them from being happy Christians.

But one thing in particular especially saddens me. It devastates me when I read letters from lonely Christians who are convinced that the shadows of their old sins are still following them. In other words, they feel God still holds their sins against them. And after telling of the evil things they did before accepting Christ, many have asked, "How could God forgive such wickedness?"

In this chapter I will show how we can survive the

guilt of what we have done in the past. Above all, I will tell how to keep from getting depressed over it. Here are some typical statements people have made in their letters:

"Depression and discouragement rule my life, and I can't control my mind."

"I would appreciate your praying for me, because my mind is really failing me. I have a problem with depression. . . . My faith is weak, and my mind is very negative."

"I am writing with the hope that perhaps you would be willing to pray for me. I have been afflicted with disabling depression for quite a long time, making it impossible, in some instances, to reason or think straight. Although I have been under medical care, doctors have not been able to help much.

"I told my last doctor that it seems at times as if some power has a hold upon me that I cannot throw off. He suggested that I talk to my minister about my problems, as I could be oppressed by the powers of darkness. Do you think such a thing could be taking place in my life? I am a God-loving person, and have been a Christian all my life."

Accepting Forgiveness

Many of God's people have a hard time accepting the fact that God has really forgiven all of their sins. Three distinct reasons hinder that acceptance, and by God's grace we can have victory over all of them.

First, we have in our fallen nature what I like to refer to as *the power of separation from God.* It consists of two distinct elements: *distrust of God* and *unbelief.* Overwhelming forces both, they have wrecked untold millions of lives through the centuries. For instance, it caused the antediluvians to refuse to enter Noah's ark and to perish in the Flood. Also it motivated the Hebrews to distrust God even though He had already delivered them from Egypt through one miracle after another. That insidious power led them to disbelieve all the good things He had told them about the Land of Promise. As a result, they died in the wilderness.

The second reason that people have some difficulty believing their sins are forgiven is that they are *spiritually starved*. When doubt entered their minds they had no spiritual stamina to resist, nothing to sustain them in a positive way. Here is an illustration. A few days ago I conversed over the phone with a woman who was quite dissatisfied with her Christian walk. As I tried to build up her confidence in God's infinite interest in our well-being, I quoted this well-known verse of Scripture: "If we confess our sins, he is faithful and just to forgive us our sins, and to cleanse us from all unrighteousness" (1 John 1:9). Immediately she asked if I could tell her where to find the passage. She had little knowledge of Scripture.

At times I plead with people to memorize Bible verses so the Holy Spirit can bring them to mind in times of need. He can then fill them with hope, faith in God, and give them power to resist evil. It encourages me when I encounter great numbers of people determined to get closer to God by memorizing His Holy Word. I can see the Holy Spirit working there, and it is wonderful.

The third reason some people find forgiveness hard to accept is that *Satan has shaken people's confidence in God's ability to forgive.*

"Demon spirits love to play games with the minds of humans," a spiritist priest told me during my days as a spirit worshiper. "They flash thoughts and images in people's minds with such delicate skill that the recipients believe them to be their own reasoning." With a great sense of satisfaction he bragged how the spirits can activate the human imagination, triggering people to like certain persons and hate others. They can cause them to experience vibrant happiness, or the direct opposite—great discouragement and depression.

When I say that we can fall under the influence of satanic suggestions, that does not mean that we are demon-possessed as is too often claimed by those involved in deliverance ministries.

As I reply to those who have written the kinds of letters I excerpted at the beginning of this chapter, I make a special effort to encourage them. I direct their attention to the fact that "(For the weapons of our warfare are not carnal, but mighty through God to the pulling down of strong holds;) casting down imaginations, and every high thing that exalteth itself against the knowledge of God, and bringing into captivity every thought to the obedience of Christ" (2 Corinthians 10:4, 5).

And I especially stress the importance of praying for the Holy Spirit to fight their spiritual battles for them. Many of those who have turned to prayer with a full understanding of what they were up against are now enjoying glorious victory over what had once been crushing problems.

Take God at His Word

Following is a letter that I wrote to a woman who faced many distresses and perplexities in her Christian walk, and felt that her problems resulted from the fact that some of her sins before her conversion had been too great for God to forgive.

"Dear Mrs. Gray:

"I read your letter of April 21 a number of times and immediately presented it before the Lord. As I did so I implored His grace for you and your family, setting forth in great detail how demonic spirits have one objective in mind—to destroy your confidence in God.

"Please do not allow yourself to lose your trust in the Lord by thinking that perhaps you are somehow deficient in your spiritual life, and therefore unable to draw closer to Him. Take courage.

" 'He hath not dealt with us after our sins; nor rewarded us according to our iniquities. For as the heaven is high above the earth, so great is his mercy toward them that fear him. As far as the east is from the west, so far hath he removed our transgressions from us. Like as a father pitieth his children, so the Lord pitieth them that fear him. For he knoweth our frame; he remembereth that we are dust' [Psalm 103:10-14].

"You stated in your letter, 'I long, oh, so much, to know His presence, His love, personally as I once did.'

"My dear sister, with God's help I can help you establish a wonderful relationship with God. But it will be one that will be solidly founded on the Word of God and not on feelings or emotions excited to some kind of an ecstasy. Its degree of excellence rests strictly on Calvary. Every morning ask the Lord Jesus to appropriate to you the merits of the blood He shed on Calvary for the remission of sin, and for Him to clothe you with the robe of His righteousness. As the apostle Paul states in his Epistle to the Philippians: 'And be found in him, not having mine own righteousness, which is of the law, but that which is through the faith of Christ, the righteousness which is of God by faith: that I may know him, and the power of his resurrection' [Philippians 3:9, 10].

"When you let Him place you in such a state, our heavenly Father views you in a whole new light. In my own Christian walk I have experienced what Paul is writing about, and it is the ultimate in closeness with God in this land of the enemy.

"Your letter especially interested me because so many of God's people struggle with the same worry. Has the Lord lost interest in them since they do not *feel* His presence as they once did? They *feel* that it is no longer easy for them to go to church, or to even have their devotions with the joy they once had. And they fear the future, concerned that they might not make it to the city of God. Furthermore, they *feel* that their lack of goodness makes it hard to live for God. As they look back upon their sinful life and the way they lived before coming to God, they become more disheartened and *feel* like giving up.

"I consider such a condition to be a spiritual malaria brought about by the enemies of all righteousness.

"It's no wonder that the Bible tells us that 'the just shall live by faith' [Habakkuk 2:4; Romans 1:17]. Or to put it another way, *take God at His word and live for Him regardless of how you may feel.*

"I know of only one way to escape the deadly spiritual malaria destroying the Christian experience of so many people. It is to memorize verses of Scripture that tell of God's love for sinners, such as John 3:16, 'For God so loved the world,' or 'Who is a God like unto thee, that pardoneth iniquity, and passeth by the transgression of the remnant of his heritage? he retaineth not his anger for ever, because he delighteth in mercy' [Micah 7:18].

"Let's consider David's life, for example.

"Think of it—here is a man who had lived life to its fullest. Most of his years were an honor to God and a glory to his nation, but not all of them. Even though he was a man after God's own heart, he still committed iniquity. For example, he coveted the wife of one of his military officers and lusted to have her as his own. Even more than that, he devised a way he could have her husband killed and out of the way. Then he rejoiced when he received the news of Uriah's death.

"To understand the full extent of the wickedness he had done, we must bear in mind that the word 'iniquity' implies having done great evil *with the full understanding that God was witnessing it all,* and that the individual didn't care a bit that God's commandments forbade such wickedness. What David did, I consider to be outright rebellion against Someone whom he claimed to love and serve. His sin was deliberate and premeditated.

"Now consider this. Humanly speaking, a man like that should not have expected God to forgive his wickedness. But because David became repentant and confessed his great iniquity, the Bible tells us that God forgave him. And I find great comfort in the thought that if He could forgive David after what he did, He is well able to forgive me, as He did 47 years ago despite the fact that I worshiped spirits and declared I hated Him.

"Years ago I memorized a large part of David's psalm of repentance (Psalm 51), particularly verses 1-3 and 10-12. These scriptures have solidified my confidence in God's willingness to forgive and, above all, to forget.

"As I have looked back on my life, the thought has often entered my mind that God could never have forgiven me. But immediately I recognized such doubt as an attempt by an evil angel to dishearten me and to have me give up on God. The only way to block such thoughts is to begin quoting verses of Scripture that tell of God's goodness and love. I especially like to quote these words of the apostle Paul:

" 'I am persuaded, that neither death, nor life, nor angels, nor principalities, nor powers, nor things present, nor things to come, nor height, nor depth, nor any other creature, shall be able to separate us from the love of God, which is in Christ Jesus our Lord' [Romans 8:38, 39].

"We must never forget the fact that as long as we live in this land of the enemy, Satan and his spirit associates will do everything possible to make us *feel* terrible. They may even torture the minds of some of us as they did to John the Baptist. If he had listened to his feelings while in prison, he would have missed out on eternal life.

"Think of it: here was a man who lived for God, had done everything possible to bring glory to Him, but now he found himself languishing in a cold and foul-smelling dungeon. I believe that you will agree with me—he would have had a good reason to give up on God.

"But like other great people of the Bible (read the eleventh chapter of Hebrews), he had fortified his mind with Scripture, and as he lifted his heart to God in prayer, the Spirit of God fortified him in right thinking, *not with feelings of ecstasy.*

"Although he lost his life for the cause of God, Jesus honored him when He said, 'Verily I say unto you, Among them that are born of women there hath not risen a greater than John the Baptist' [Matthew 11:11].

"You may not agree with me, but I am inclined to believe that the Spirit of God is preparing you for a special work, one that will demand that you walk by faith and not by sight or feelings of ecstasy. The time will soon be here when God's commandment-keeping churches will need individuals who will walk by faith *only*, no matter what.

"At that time God's people will need encouragement from such special people. People whom the Spirit of God has already led to fortify themselves by memorizing the Word of God. And it could very well be that Jesus wants you to be one of those powerful people.

"It is my firm conviction that, by the grace of Him who went the way of Calvary to accomplish our salvation, you will be made a great overcomer."

Since then I have corresponded with others struggling with the same doubt that distressed Mrs. Gray's life. I am pleased to say that the Holy Spirit has blessed the lives of many of them with hope and faith. They have found peace in the Lord and a new vision for the future. A number of them later phoned me about the changes in their lives.

The Lord has given us beautiful minds and blessed us with the capacity to form in them images of things not present to the senses. God has endowed us with the ability to create new ideas or to combine old ones in new ways. That crowning element is our imagination.

Let us always watch and pray over it with all possible diligence lest Satan injure or distort it. Only through divine help can those tragic men and women who write to me overcome the terrible discouragement and misery that Satan and this sin-filled world heaps upon them. Christ is eagerly waiting to give us through the Holy Spirit incredible power, incredible victory, and incredible joy. Our lives will then give Him incredible glory.